REFORMING DEMOCRACIES

LEONARD HASTINGS SCHOFF MEMORIAL LECTURES

UNIVERSITY SEMINARS

LEONARD HASTINGS SCHOFF MEMORIAL LECTURES

*The University Seminars at Columbia University sponsor an annual series
of lectures, with the support of the Leonard Hastings Schoff and Suzanne Levick
Schoff Memorial Fund. A member of the Columbia faculty is
invited to deliver before a general audience three lectures on a topic of his or
her choosing. Columbia University Press publishes the lectures.*

David Cannadine, **The Rise and Fall of Class in Britain**   1993

Charles Larmore, **The Romantic Legacy**   1994

Saskia Sassen, **Sovereignty Transformed: States and the
New Transnational Actors**   1995

Robert Pollack, **The Faith of Biology and
the Biology of Faith: Order, Meaning, and Free
Will in Modern Medical Science**   2000

Ira Katznelson, **Desolation and Enlightenment:
Political Knowledge After the Holocaust,
Totalitarianism, and Total War**   2003

Lisa Anderson, **Pursuing Truth, Exercising Power:
Social Science and Public Policy in the
Twenty-first Century**   2003

Partha Chatterjee, **The Politics of the Governed:
Reflections on Popular Politics in Most of the World**   2004

David Rosand, **The Invention of Painting in America**   2004

George Rupp, **Globalization Challenged: Conviction,
Conflict, Community**   2007

Lesley A. Sharp, **Bodies, Commodities,
and Technologies**   2007

Robert Hanning, **Serious Play: Desire and Authority in the
Poetry of Ovid, Chaucer, and Ariosto**   2010

Douglas A. Chalmers

REFORMING DEMOCRACIES

SIX FACTS ABOUT POLITICS
THAT DEMAND A NEW AGENDA

COLUMBIA UNIVERSITY PRESS
NEW YORK

COLUMBIA UNIVERSITY PRESS

Publishers Since 1893

New York   Chichester, West Sussex

cup.columbia.edu

Library of Congress Cataloging-in-Publication Data

Chalmers, Douglas A.

Reforming democracies : six facts about politics that demand a new
agenda / Douglas A. Chalmers.

p. cm. — (Leonard Hastings Schoff memorial lectures)

Includes bibliographical references and index.

ISBN 978-0-231-16294-4 (cloth : alk. paper)

ISBN 978-0-231-53105-4 (e-book)

1. Democracy.   2. Representative government and representation.
I. Title.

JC423.C51245 2012

312.8—dc23

2012024444

COVER DESIGN: Thomas Beck Stvan

CONTENTS

PREFACE

A half century of studying the establishment or reestablishment of democratic institutions in Europe after World War II and in Latin America in the last third of the twentieth century has left me with puzzles. Certain facts came up again and again that distorted the analysis and stood in the way of analytically simple recipes for enhancing democracy. I found myself studying the impact of clientelism and personal dependence, the presence of foreigners wheeling and dealing, the volatility of nongovernmental organizations, the way "crazy" (or new) ideas change the actors and their engagement, and the "back rooms" where decisions are "really" made—all of which are outside or contrary to the usual standards for democracy, but in some form often have had a significant and positive role to play. They are too much a part of the systems to be "banned." They need attention in any effort to assess democracy—and to reform it.

These facts are

- The political importance of noncitizens inside a country
- The similar importance of people in other jurisdictions
- The rapidity of the rise and fall of a large number of civil society associations

- The continuing importance of personal ties
- The crucial role of ideas (when our worldview emphasizes material interests)
- The enormous range of places within a system where consequential decisions about law and policy are made

The political processes pointed to by these six facts were being treated as marginal to the question of what makes a system democratic, but I have come to believe that they are, in fact, central. Democracy depends on shaping them, the way that sixteenth- to twentieth-century Europe shaped its politics by institutionalizing elections, representative legislatures, separation of powers, civil rights, and political party systems in order to pull together the nation-state, deal with uncontrolled monarchs and aristocrats, and, eventually, cope with class conflict. The contemporary challenges demand that actions pointed to by the six facts—which have always existed, but are assuming new importance—be regulated and guided (i.e., institutionalized) if democratic outcomes will be more than the accidents of good luck. We need a new agenda of institutional reform.

I will argue that as a result of these six problems, we must think about additional kinds of institutions, around three headings:

- Institutions that regulate the processes of creating and reshaping decision-making networks that are, in fact, constructed ad hoc
- Institutions that regulate the way we mobilize, vet, debate, and deploy the facts, theories, and interpretations that shape decision making
- Institutions that shape the way noncitizens are linked to and, therefore, represented in the process of making particular decisions

This book is only a beginning. It points to important political and social processes and conditions that have too often been assumed away by reformers. It suggests where reforms are needed, but only begins to specify the appropriate democratic institutions.

In the introduction, I argue that institutional reform is necessary. Then, in part I, I define "representative democracy" in a way not tied to the existing models of political institutions so that we can see how the activities referred to as the six facts fit into a more relevant model. The definition points to three parts of the process:

- Identifying "the people" to be represented
- Organizing the elites that make the decisions for "the people"
- Creating the links that connect the elites to "the people"

I sketch the reigning models of institutions conventionally assumed to be crucial to making these three elements work democratically. Parts II to IV discuss aspects of modern politics not embraced by the established models. There are two such aspects each for "the people," the decision makers, and the links between them. The conclusion offers a few guidelines to new thinking.

This book is an outgrowth of lectures in the Leonard Hastings Schoff Memorial Lecture series sponsored by the University Seminars of Columbia University in November 2007 under the title "Representative Government Without Representatives." I want particularly to thank Robert Belknap for his support and encouragement. I also owe a debt to my students in a seminar on this topic, my colleagues in the Department of Political Science, the anonymous reviewer, and friends who have demonstrated how risky it is to reconceptualize an entrenched set of understandings.

REFORMING DEMOCRACIES

INTRODUCTION

WHY DO WE NEED INSTITUTIONAL REFORM?

Democratic institutions are under attack in even the most "advanced" democracies. They must be rebuilt and repaired. Reforming the institutions of democratic government is essential to overcoming serious faults and creating more just societies. Reforms are proposed and adopted with great regularity. But they often are marginal or fail not only because of incompetence or malfeasance—the usual explanations—but also because, I suggest, they do not address some highly relevant sets of norms, practices, laws, and procedures; in other words, they do not address the right institutions. My argument is that knowledge of and reform of the institutions that regulate important aspects of politics and that are left out of the usual discussions are required to deal with the current discontents. To construct enduring, genuinely democratic regimes, it is necessary to represent the interests of noncitizens acting within a country and in other jurisdictions, to deal with the rapidly changing civil society, to promote beneficial personal links, to encourage useful information and effective deliberation on policy and law, and to manage the myriad decision networks that constitute the political system.

First, however, why do we have to worry?

The ideal of democracy is so strong that almost all governments now claim to be, or to be on the way to being, democracies. Yet criticism of the performance of even the most advanced democracies has been steady and increasing. Democracy is the approved ideal of governance, and thus it is no surprise that demands become stronger and more focused on making democracy work (as opposed to junking it for "something better"). But it is surprising that more progress has not been made, given the enormous arsenal of skills that are applied to the analysis of reforms by politicians, academics, bloggers, legal authorities, and pundits.

The problems are manifest and often taken for granted as "the way things are," but the costs are great. Many of the concerns are similar to those that the standard institutions of representative democracy, which evolved in the great constitution-writing period in the seventeenth and eighteenth centuries, were designed to combat. They stand as the failures of representative democracy.

• *Inequality*: Shifting power from the royal court to elected legislatures was meant to put political power in the hands of those who would dismantle privilege (or assign it more rationally), yet excessive inequality not only persists but increases. The idea that everyone is represented in a democratic system has been widely proclaimed and celebrated, yet dramatic inequality is notable in income, education, health care, financial security, and many other dimensions. Some inequalities—such as those based on working-class status, race, and gender—have been weakened, but hardly eliminated. Some attributes remain as "legitimate" reasons for unequal treatment, such as being young, being disabled, and being a criminal. New or expanded old categories—migrants, ethnic minorities, and refugees—often become new underclasses. Once hidden differences, such as sexual orientation and drug use, become grounds for discrimination. The justice of some inequalities is defended by most, and the definition of "equality" calls up endless discussion. Good representative processes would ideally identify all these groups clearly, treat each justly, promote respect for each, and equalize opportunities and rewards where appropriate. We are a long way from such a state.

• *Reckless executives*: Liberal democratic government arguably emerged as a counterforce to the recklessness of monarchs of the seventeenth through nineteenth centuries who pursued fruitless wars abroad, religious persecution at home, or grandiose personal projects. The conversion of advisory councils, laws, and courts into sovereign legislatures, constitutions with bills of rights, and independent judiciaries was predicated on the belief that representative institutions would act as watchdogs over executives on behalf of the welfare of the people.

Yet the failed colonial experiences of the nineteenth and twentieth centuries, the reckless slide into weakness of the European powers faced with the rise of Hitler, the rise of Nazism itself, and the recent experience of the reckless wars fought by the United States in Vietnam, Iraq, and Afghanistan point to drastic limits on the capacity of the representative political process to prevent the escalation of "mistakes" and "tentative efforts to solve problems" into disasters. Many Americans are justly proud that the mobilization against the Vietnam War contributed to its termination and that constitutional and electoral processes brought new leadership to Washington after the dramatic failures of the George W. Bush administration. But in both cases, years passed during which the actions of the president failed to accomplish their declared goals and, more important, failed to promote the public interest. The system may ultimately right itself, but it was unable to stop the waste of an unacceptable number of lives and an enormous amount of treasure, and the loss of the credibility and moral stature of the United States in the world. The most damaging processes are being terminated, but any organization that takes so long to correct such egregious errors and that proves unable to absorb new information about its own failures has to be considered at least a partial failure.

• *Corruption*: Creating representative government was part of a shift of power from the elites to the people, presumably weakening the impunity of powerful leaders who used public positions to satisfy their greed and self-interest. Nevertheless, those who have the power to make decisions that affect a very large number of people—whether formally public or, perhaps more sensationally, private (such as executives of major companies or financial institutions)—are able to amass enormous fortunes using public power. Sometimes this takes the form of old-fashioned secret manipulation of regulations, sale of public offices and licenses, and the like. Sometimes, however, the corruption lies in legal maneuvers to avoid taxes, to engage in insider trading, and to create financial "instruments"—like the Ponzi scheme and devices to bet on and, in fact, trigger failure—that stretch the laws in ways that cannot be prosecuted as corruption, but use public power for personal gain with no corresponding public advantage. A government for the people should be the instrument through which such corruption is outlawed and punished. Yet it continues—even flourishes.

• *Weakness in mobilizing for action*: The recent recession drives home the fact that contemporary democratic systems have a great deal of difficulty in avoiding the costs associated with sharp swings in economic activity. The phenomenon, based on contagious reductions in purchasing and producing, is treated almost as a force of nature. Steps taken to avoid the swings are tentative and contested. Disagreements about the policies and competing strategies to survive during a recession are not dealt with and block consensus and action. In this case, at least, collective action that involves applying the right information and mobilizing energies to act collectively is hesitant, slow acting, and sometimes counterproductive.

How might we respond to these problems? Perhaps there is nothing to do beyond exhorting our representatives to greater vigilance. Corruption, we might say, is always with us. Inequality is inevitable, injustices should be addressed only at the margins, and it is in the nature of any government that executive authorities may engage in reckless, badly conceived actions—and periodic elections are the means to hold them accountable. Democracies have long been held to be inherently incapable of decisive action. Or, perhaps, as some hard-core libertarians might say, whether the problem is serious and fixable or not, it is not the government's role to address it. Many suggest that recessions are inevitable and have to work themselves out.

Most people would agree, I believe, that an effort should be made to correct the failures of representative democracy. But perhaps institutional reform is too slow, uncertain, and costly. Thus a variety of actions other than institutional reform are often proposed rhetorically and sometimes seriously.

• One common reaction is to demand new policies—new laws and uses of resources—rather than basic political reforms. Particularly when rhetoric is at a premium—for example, during election campaigns—politicians argue that righting the wrongs of the system can be accomplished by well-crafted policies, not reforms of representative institutions. Programs and laws could solve specific problems. Elect us, and we will pass laws that will bring corrupt officials to trial, attack inequality through redistributive and anti-discrimination laws, and thwart a rogue executive by blocking his access to resources, prosecuting his advisers, and withdrawing funding for his adventures. The incumbent president or legislators may not know what to do to avoid the costs of a recession, for example, but it is not the institutions of democratic government that are at fault, but the ability of those in charge of making and implementing policy to perceive what has to be done and summon the political smarts to implement solutions.

• A second, more drastic answer is a call for revolution. Problems like financial and social inequality and economic downturns are serious, it is held, and cannot be remedied by normal politics. The business cycle is built into the free-enterprise system and can be dealt with only by abolishing that system. Inequality results from cultural prejudices and/or is created by the economic necessities of capitalism. These structural failures are beyond the reach of any existing government, which was established to support the prevailing racial-cultural-nationalist prejudices or existing economic systems. The only way to deal with them is massive destruction and reconstruction. Historically, a frequent way people think about inequality is that only overturning social structures and the institutions that support them can resolve such problems.[1] Eliminating corruption may take a religious awakening. Out-of-control executives can be handled only by rooting out the entrenched, conspiratorial cabals that are guiding them and installing more righteous advisers.

• A third strategy, which may be considered a surgical revolution, is the social-movement model. While a total overhaul of the sociopolitical structure may be a dangerously blunt instrument of change, the sources of social and economic problems are so integral to the entrenched political practices that a dramatic confrontation is necessary. Popular demonstrations and boycotts of companies led by corrupt executives, marches and civil disobedience to highlight inequality, and public shows of defiance of political leaders may force reconsideration of faulty policies. Marches by the unemployed or confrontations in town-hall meetings may compel political leaders to take action against a recession. Although social movements may take many forms, the words "mobilization," "contestation," and "challenge" suggest the kind of shock that could bring about change.[2] These approaches strive to and sometimes succeed in altering the conditions under which the representative institutions work, by awakening the people, mobilizing them to vote for change, or transforming hegemonic ideas. The implication is that reform of the institutions is secondary or can result most readily from taking to the streets—literally or figuratively.

• A fourth response to social and economic problems is the "dictator" solution (taking the name from ancient practice). It classically involves giving all power to a single leader, but these days it would more likely subject a government to a superior power that could guide it "correctly." Historically, this remedy has been tried by the military undertaking a coup d'état, a religious authority asserting its God-given power, an international commission (such as one urging the jurisdiction of a human rights authority), a central government intervening in a state or province in a federal system, or a colonial power shouldering its "burden" to "civilize the natives."

Each of these responses—legislate problems away, smash and rebuild the system, dramatically confront the powers that be, import a deus ex machina— may be rational in some circumstances. But the failures of democracy are long term and persistent. They are not likely to be solved in a single blow, no matter how heavy or well placed. They require long-lasting remedies, and the reform of political institutions may be the only enduring solution.

Perhaps, though, the reform of political institutions may not require rebuilding them and rewriting constitutional documents, but simply affecting their context to make them work better. For example, media reform can improve the public's awareness of issues before they vote or even when interest groups lobby. The vast expansion of available information is accompanied by overload and extraordinary levels of manipulation. So there is a sense that the exposure of such manipulation or guidance in how the media operate will produce better-informed citizens, which will lead to better voting and more savvy poll taking. Another familiar example is get-out-the-vote campaigns. Yet another is encouraging investigative reporting by the media. It might weaken corruption by exposing it, for example. In the United States, it has certainly redefined the nature of corruption, which now includes marital infidelity and sexual misconduct as well as material gain. These are, no doubt, good steps to take, although they seem limited in dealing with the failures of the political system.

Changing the behavior of such a politically relevant sector as the media would change something, but the direction is not so certain. For example, the dramatic increase in sources of news and information apparently realizes the principle of freedom of speech; according to the theory made famous by John Stuart Mill, the more voices heard, the more likely the truth will be found—and, presumably, the better the policies crafted.[3] Whether the expansion of the media produces better or worse policy, though, depends on how information is fed into the decision-making process. A cacophony of ideas and proposals may stall or confuse, rather than enlighten. If certain interests have access to the media and others do not, that would have a deleterious impact. If ideas and information enter the decision-making process in such a way that they influence only "image makers" and not decision makers, there may be no effect on the output of policy.

More complex are efforts to attack inequality based on gender and race through public campaigns to change perceptions of "the other." Transforming the culture in regard to such issues is essential for any long-term solution, but the impact can and often is blunted by contrary moves and is likely to take a long time.

Another strategy to make existing institutions work better is to promote the growth of a vibrant civil society, often seen as a step in making the work of parties and legislatures more favorable to the interests of broader segments of the population. Stimulating the development of civic associations, volunteer organizations, charitable institutions, and social groups often has been held to enhance the operation of the classic institutions of representative government. Alexis de Tocqueville regarded them as combating the excessive turn into private life that he called "individualism" and as motivating participation in formal political institutions.[4] Many saw "pluralism," which implied a large number of interest groups, as a counter to the vicious partisanship that led to the rise of fascism and Nazism and the outbreak of World War II. More recently, people have noted the significant role of civil society associations in exposing and dismantling the authoritarian regimes in many Third World countries and have concluded that they were a force for democracy. Civic organizations have been seen to have a role in encouraging the trust necessary to act civilly with others in a modern political system. The vibrancy of civil society has been a common theme in writings that promote democracy or counter its problems.[5]

But, again, how are civil society associations connected to the political process in a way that enhances democracy? There is often a huge gap between the presence of many groups in society and the process of decision making in the public interest. It is a simple model to imagine them as clamoring for good policies. But if we are looking for how civil society is organized into an ongoing presence in the political process of making decisions, and what makes its impact more or less democratic, the answers are not clear. Strategies for influencing decision makers include raising public awareness, lobbying, and testifying before legislative committees, but what would make a system work in the public interest and not be a field day for special interests (however virtuous) is a great deal less apparent.[6]

Another common recipe for making political systems operate more democratically is the active promotion of social and political rights. It is undeniable that an objective of democratic government can be legitimately expressed in these terms and that enhancing the rights to participate and freely express opinions has a good deal to do with making a government more responsive. If we are focused on the output of policy, however, there remains the question of how such freedoms may improve the policy making of the government. The "free market" of ideas suggests a positive view of the results, but it is more difficult to say how this might be connected to the actual adoption of policy.[7] It may be true that improving the freedoms of the people is a good in itself, and like the economy, it is assumed that freedoms will yield efficient outcomes, but like the economy much depends on the "regulations" in force. Similarly, rights are a beginning, but not a complete building block of a democratic system.

All these good ideas, then, skirt the question of the reform of political institutions: the norms, laws, and accepted procedures that shape how the laws and policies are decided, how decision makers relate to the people, and who the people are. This may seem unsurprising. The political institutions have been the subject of inquiry by observers, participants, constitution drafters, and political scientists for many years, even centuries. So it may seem as if there is nothing much to do about institutions.

This pessimism about institutional reform has two sources. The first, often noted, is that the endless tinkering with electoral regulations, legislative rules, the party system, the balance of power, and the other institutions in the classic definition of government has in fact not produced dramatic changes. The second, less well recognized, is that observers, participants, constitution drafters, and political scientists have not focused on all the relevant institutions.

In this book, I argue that if institutional reform is needed to correct these faults (and I very much believe that it is), we have a much too narrow and static vision of the institutions that require reform. We have focused on revising or perfecting the institutions associated with the impressive and even glorious tradition of representative government founded essentially in the anti-monarchical European revolutions of the seventeenth and eighteenth centuries, and the incipient or real class wars of the nineteenth and twentieth. I believe that this emphasis is misleading. However natural it seems to equate "democratic institutions" with elections, legislatures, party systems, and control of executives, they are only part of the picture.

I have spoken of this misperception of democratic institutions as problematic because it blocks steps to deal with the failures noted at the beginning of this introduction. But there is another consequence of these blinders: the misjudgments that Americans make about other countries. For example, why do some countries, like Brazil, that seem to have broken institutions of representative democracy nevertheless do so well.[8] Even more problematic will be the effort to decide when China is becoming democratic, since its institutions seem so fundamentally contrary to the Western liberal tradition. In many such countries, because of their histories or the timing of their democratization, the classic institutions of Western democracy are unlikely to be founded or likely to be counterproductive to operate. China, Russia, Brazil, and now the countries of the Middle East in the midst of the so-called Arab Spring come to mind. The questions have to be changed from, Have they replicated the institutions of the West? to, Do their institutions replicate the hard-won *results* in the West? It may well be that China cannot be considered representative of its people until its citizens have free, contested elections, but our ability to assess the progress the country has made toward the goals of democracy will be lost if we do not have a vision of institutions that includes how the policies of China—and other countries—are shaped by the desires and needs of its people. Without some notion of these crucial processes serious mistakes will be made.

If we are to look at the real world of politics and proceed without adopting the conventional wisdom about what institutions are relevant to the reform of representative democracy, we will need a conception of what representative democratic institutions are in order to use it as a lens. In chapter 1, I present such a view. Then utilizing this tool, I discuss the conventional models of democratic institutions to establish them as a foil for a new conception.

The rest of the book discusses six political facts. All of them concern the interaction of the decision makers and the population, the relationship that is at the heart of what we consider democratic. Two of these facts pertain to the people, the demos, whose interests must be taken into account (part II). Citizens, however they are defined, are not the only people whose interests have to be engaged, whose compliance is required, and whose cooperation is desirable. The other group that is important to decision making I will call quasi-citizens. Two facts deal with the links between the people and the decision makers (part III). They suggest that we have to take into account not only the multiplicity of interests, but their constant reconfiguration, and those expressed not only through formal organizations, but also through personal networks. And, finally, two facts concern the organization of decision making itself (part IV). They suggest that decision making both is heavily deliberative and occurs in many different places in the political system.

PART I
THE CONCEPTS

RETHINKING THE INSTITUTIONS OF REPRESENTATIVE DEMOCRACY

Significant reform of institutions is complex even when we know which institutions need rectification, but it is likely to be fruitless or produce unexpected results when we do not know. Too often, we assume that the identity of the institutions of representative democracy is a given and the only question is what reforms will work. We should be asking what processes are important and what rules, norms, and laws regulate them. In other words, it is necessary to *discover* the institutions of representative democracy before reforming them.

To explore what should be included, we start with a description of the political processes that are or should be regulated by such institutions, then sketch the series of conventional conceptions of democratic institutions we use, and finally point to aspects that seem to be left out.

DEFINITIONS AND CONVENTIONAL ANSWERS

What are the "parts" of decision making in a representative system? Regimes are particular configurations of processes that collectively overcome (or succumb to or ignore) uncertainties and conflicts, decide on the laws that are enforced within a territory, and make policies that determine the use of resources of the state. When we speak of a "representative democracy," we are talking about a particular form of the institutions that shape the outcomes of those decision-making processes.

For the purposes of this book, the standard I posit for the outcomes of a political system that make it worthy of the label "democratic" is that the laws and policies promote the interests of the people. A successful democratic system is one in which the output of laws and policies is favorable to the people. It is a simple definition, but I believe that it points to something all would agree to: a democratic system must serve the people. And if we combine this definition with the crucial empirical assumption that a high level of interaction with the people—including accountability to them—is required for the decision makers to know and act on what is good for the people, it embraces many of the important meanings of the word "democracy" as currently used.[1]

Other ways of specifying what is democratic are possible. A common one related to the liberal tradition appears to move in a different direction. It is whether the rule of law prevails and the fundamental rights of individuals are protected. Born out of the struggle to prevent tyrants, monarchs, and aristocrats from oppressing those in their power, the great victory of democratic movements was and still is establishing limits on what the people in power can do, for which laws and rights are instrumental. Establishing those limits are absolutely essential for democracy. Other problems than those discussed in the introduction require respect for rights and ways to prevent the officials of the state, politicians, and even elected deputies from exploiting others, riding roughshod over their rights, and enhancing their power for selfish purposes. The liberal qualities of democracy are essential.

But to deal with the failures of established democracies discussed in the introduction—gross inequality, executive recklessness, corruption, and stalemate—more is needed than preventing acts that limit freedom. Governments need the capacity to act in favor of the people, not just to refrain from acting against them. Each of the four failures requires not only respect for the law, but the ability to bring together citizens who will analyze problems, agree on steps toward a solution, and move the collective resources of the people to realize laws and policies that will benefit them. Fighting inequality needs intelligent policies not only for redistributing resources, but for structuring opportunities and influencing public opinion. Defeating executive recklessness requires not only holding leaders responsible after the fact, but finding the means to generate a meaningful discussion of a situation to which the executive is responding. Curbing corruption demands not only laws against it and punishments for their violation, but strategies to make the opportunities more scarce and the payoffs less attractive. And stalemate is, literally, the inability to act.

To approach the challenge of reforming institutions so they can confront the failures mentioned in the introduction, we have to think about the processes that produce policies and laws, and then investigate what institutions might regulate them in a fashion that would tend to promote the interests of the people.

Politics is about collective action. Democratic politics is action that realizes the will of the people. It is true that one aspect of what is in the interest of the people is to establish rights and the rule of law. But without the capacity to act in the people's interest, that goal would not be realized.

SOME MISLEADING DIRECTIONS FROM THE WORDS "DEMOCRACY" AND "REPRESENTATIVE"

To begin by clearing some potential obstacles, two seemingly logical and commonly taken directions for investigating democratic institutions are misleading. Commonly used words always have a cloud of meanings around them, and the definitions associated with the two words naming this type of regime— "democracy" and "representative"—are loaded with traps. First, "democracy."

In a democratic regime, the demos—the people—rule, have the "last word," and thus are sovereign because their welfare is the standard against which the regime is measured. So much is agreed. But many start from the etymology of the word or rely on classical definitions, which suggest that in a democratic regime, the people rule directly. One of the reasons why democracy had such a bad name for centuries, and still does for some people, is that ordinary people are not interested in or suited for leading. But because democracy is taken to be direct rule of the people, that fact is challenged or overlooked, and the reformers concentrate on involving everyday people in the actual business of governing. If the bottom line is the welfare of the people, the argument goes, engaging people in the everyday work of government will improve the quality of policy and laws to the people's benefit. A perfect democracy, they say, would be one in which all the citizens participate in making decisions and, perhaps, in carrying them out.[2]

But the relationship between the level of participation and the democratic payoff in the decisions made is an empirical question, not a definitional one. Broad participation sometimes does produce policies more favorable to the people, but other times it does not. The result clearly depends on more than the number of people involved. I will not try to spell out which conditions that encourage participation (e.g., organizing get-out-the-vote programs, fostering town hall meetings with legislators, promoting blogs on important issues) produce better results for the people.[3] It is an important question, but not the task at hand. Direct public participation in decision making is a possible contributor to outcomes favorable to the welfare of the people, even a probable contributor to it, but it is not the same as "democratic" in the meaning I am using, which makes central the output of laws and policies being in the public interest. Public participation does not define this kind of democracy; political processes leading to public welfare does.

In order to talk about the regulation of a political system to maximize the welfare of the people, we must focus on what makes the people who run the system act in the popular interest. The people must always be present to the decision makers, but "present" means different things. All modern political systems are representative in the sense that some citizens act for others. The question is not whether the people do the actual ruling, but whether the system includes processes that compel the decision makers to frame policies and laws that benefit the people.[4]

If direct rule by the people is only a partial description of what goes on in a democratic system, a standard, conventional supplement is to say that such a regime is "representative," meaning that some rule "for" the people, implying a key relationship between the representatives and the people. And while that seems straightforward, "representative" is another complicated and potentially misleading word. The institutions we are looking for are those that make the laws and politics they produce serve the people's interests. And we can say that if it is working, the ensemble of decision makers represents the people. But that task does not specify how they are connected. It is easy to assume that it does and to slip from a general statement about the government representing the people to a much more specific and restrictive one that asserts that the government is, or should be, made up of representatives, each of whom represents a particular set of people.

Colloquially, we identify a representative system with one composed of persons elected to "represent" geographic units or political parties. When we hear the term "representative government," we commonly think of elected deputies and their relationship to their constituents. A popular image of representation is akin to the model of legal representation, where a lawyer represents a client in a principal–agent relationship. Thus rather than regarding the system as representing all the people, the emphasis is on the nature of the relationship between an elected official and his or her constituency or, perhaps more broadly, between any advocate, lobbyist, or political actor and those who support him or her because of his or her identification with their interests in contrast to those of others.[5]

Strengthening the temptation to use the word "representative" in this way is the historic fact that some of the achievements of democracy have come only when outsiders found their champions and fought their way into the system. In some cases, only with the incorporation of representatives bound to particular repressed groups did governments even approach representing "everybody." The classic examples of such a challenge—the fights against entrenched aristocrats, capitalists, military leaders, or theocratic rulers, ruling in their own interest—point to very important historical moments. The first thought in a "democratic transition" turns often to the people taking power from the autocrat through their elected representatives in a legislature: the Third Estate in the French Revolution, the middle class in the revolution in Russia in 1905, and the Social Democratic Party and the workers in the Weimar Republic in Germany. The notion of revolution, so central to the founding of democratic states, seems to imply the necessity of installing representatives specifically for the underprivileged, the disadvantaged, the less powerful, minorities, or repressed majorities.[6]

Transferring this historical sequence into pointers to the institutions that link leaders and the population and thus into criteria for judging the level of democracy even in well-institutionalized democratic systems has always been a temptation. Major social groups often do not have someone in power who speaks for them, leaving many opportunities for "tribunes of the oppressed." But translating historical achievements into criteria for analyzing how democracies operate does not always work. At some point, we have to look at other problems in addition to new groups that are totally excluded. We turn to understanding how groups already involved in the political system are in fact treated and how their interests are balanced with those of other groups in society. Representative democracy may suffer from a failure to bring in "outsiders," but it also may suffer from the failure to balance, integrate, and harmonize those who are already "in the system."

Once groups are in the system—say, African Americans, women, new immigrants, and gays, not to mention seniors, small-business owners, farmers, oil companies, investment banks, environmentalists, sports enthusiasts, and on and on—it makes no sense to look for a link between each and every group and "its" man or woman, its representative in the system. Rendering it even more unlikely is the fact that the interests, and therefore the groups, change constantly. What makes all the difference is if all those interests are heard seriously and in a timely manner and given their due weight. Getting more women or African Americans into government is only the beginning. To outline the processes that promote representative democracy, therefore, it is not enough to look at the relations between deputies and constituents, between agents and principals. Whether the government as a whole rules in the interests of all the people is the central concern, not whether some actors specifically argue for particular groups in society. The processes that link decision makers and the people are much more complicated than those between a deputy and his or her constituents.[7]

An additional problem with a definition of "representative democracy" on those narrow lines is that along with the actors in government who are representatives in the specific sense of being elected to a legislature by particular constituencies, there are many other actors who play a role in determining the outcome of the decision process. They include members of the executive (elected and not) and the judiciary, staffs of legislators and other officials, prominent advisers both inside and outside the formal offices, regular participants in discussions in the media, public intellectuals, and anyone who regularly contributes to making (or blocking) decisions. However central the legislators are to the process of making law, much regulation—decree law as well as wide areas of economic, military, cultural, and other policy—is strongly shaped by these "others."

Considering all these other actors as simply ancillary to the decision-making process that "really" goes on in the legislature among representatives cuts out a great deal of the political process we are interested in. A parallel idea—that these "others" fill mostly "executive" roles and the elected representatives of constituencies are the only democratic actors in the system—places a responsibility on the elected representatives that they are not capable of fulfilling even under the best circumstances.[8]

The people and the links that are established between the people and the decision makers are far too complex and changeable to be summarized in a simple group–individual relationship. Particularly in the light of the six conditions that form the basis of this book, any attempt to "freeze" the role of political actors as agents of single interests is potentially very destructive.

The government is not a set of actors, each of whom is representative of a single interest. It is a set of processes, and it is that set of processes that is representative (or not), certainly not just the elected members of the legislature. Representative democracy involves those decision-making processes that act for the people, in their interest.[9]

In this book, then, the word "democracy" does not mean a government in which the people actually carry out ruling functions, and the word "representative" does not mean a government of agents or deputies. Representative democracy is a system in which processes carried out by a minority make, implement, and enforce the decisions for the collectivity. It is "representative rule" as opposed to "direct rule by the people" because only a minority is actually ruling. It is "representative" not because of representatives but because the ensemble of decision makers and the processes that connect them to the people produce results that are in the interest of those people.

We need a word for demos-oriented interactive government, but it is not obvious what term would be less misleading than "representative democracy."[10] So I shall use the term "representative democracy" even though both of its constituent words are potentially misleading.

THE ELEMENTS OF REPRESENTATIVE DEMOCRACY: DECISIONS, PEOPLE, AND LINKS

Reduced to its essentials, there are three elements of politics crucial to representative democracy:

- The processes that lead to law or policy choices among those able to shape state action
- The people whose interests are to be brought into the calculation of those decisions
- The communication between those people and the actors who make the choices

The first element is the interactions among the groups that make the choices. Those outputs of the political process are ultimately the result of many-sided decision-making processes, involving many people. I will lump them under the term "decision making." Steps in the process include specifying problems, making proposals, assembling information about contexts, discovering "best practices," envisioning likely scenarios and outcomes, identifying and linking stakeholders, discussing and bargaining, deciding among alternatives, and promulgating, implementing, and reviewing outcomes.[11] All the decision makers are linked to processes that lead to the final conversion of proposals into law or the commitment of resources to implement a policy.

The way in which decision makers process information and define, redefine, and resolve problems is crucial. A set of decision makers may be inundated with information, demands, and pressures from the people, but that will not automatically produce good decisions. The payoff is how all these communications combine to produce decisions, laws, and policies. (We return to this in part IV.)

The second major element of a working political system concerns the processes that identify "the people" whose interests are (or are not) being promoted. They are commonly called "citizens." On a theoretical level, the concept is constantly being reformulated in the literature. The debate is inconclusive in part because the term has both a legal and a theoretical reality. The legal status of "citizen" varies from system to system, and the relationship of the legal status of "citizen" to other characteristics of individuals is not agreed on. The complex and partial integration of the member nations of the European Union has given rise to much of the contemporary discussion because "the people" of one historic country do not simply become "the people" of the EU in the same way that their ancestors did when the nation-states of Europe were founded. Identity, territoriality, participation, nationalistic sentiments, obligations for service, and taxation all become possible bases for "citizenship." So there are many compromises, distinctions, and redefinitions.[12] (We return to this in part II.)

Most crucial for our discussion of representative government is the third set of processes that make up a political system: the links between the decision makers and the people. When decision makers wish to pass laws and adopt policies for the people's benefit, one might assume (and dictators allege) that they can, on their own or with the help of "experts," determine what is best and act on it. But there is no way that decision makers can know what is in the people's interest without ongoing communication with the people about their wants, the conditions under which they live, the consequences for them of various proposed actions, and their likely reactions.[13] That even the most sensitive dictator cannot know what is good for the people without constant interaction is in part because the people's interests change, but more because the context of each decision is new and judging the people's interest depends not only on their preferences but on the possibilities, the new consequence of this or that choice, and the impact of actions taken by others. Knowing "what the people want" requires constant interaction. Conversely, there is no way that the people can know what is in their interest without information about possibilities, opportunities, and threats—which decision makers often are in a good position to tell them about.

The informational links are thus two-directional.[14] From the bottom up, so to speak, decision makers are made aware of the preferences and perspectives of the people, as well as information about their situation and theories about what actions would or would not improve it. Such communication may involve personal visits by constituents and lobbyists to decision makers, public-opinion polls, Internet messages, mass demonstrations, media coverage, terrorist attacks, op-ed pieces, visits by officials to local gatherings, meetings with experts, and many other things. Elections and public-opinion polls provide some information, but they are clearly only a small part and generally very blunt instruments for understanding what action to take.

Decision makers not only receive information, but from the top down they outline alternatives, discuss obstacles, "sell" certain policies, try to obfuscate or clarify the issues, give the people a framework for understanding (or misperceiving) what is at stake, and the like. Observers and commentators—including researchers, think tanks, academics, op-ed writers, policy shops, and bloggers—are folded into the decision-making apparatus. The discussions, debates, and conflicts always shape public opinion, as well as attitudes among decision makers.

These interactions may be a serious dialogue between the people and the politicians or an exercise in advertising, obfuscation, and salesmanship. At some point, people and elites may arrive at a consensus on what is going on and what to do about it, they may just keep on talking or shouting, or they may turn to violence. Agreement may be an exercise in mutual self-delusion (which yields results as bad as those from willful ignoring of popular needs).[15] One of the common propositions in discussing representative systems is that the wishes of the people should command. But it is the wishes after consideration and reflection and discussion.[16] Overcoming the possibility of mutual delusion is as important as avoiding selfish behavior on the part of decision makers or ungrounded anti-elite actions by masses of people.

The links are complex for another reason, too. We are speaking of democracy, which requires that decisions be made in the public interest. If there is any tendency for decision makers not to rule in the people's interest—to reward themselves or simply to be incompetent—the links must go beyond conveying information to include the means for keeping them in line. Thus there are two broad sets of intertwined connections between decision makers and the people: the exchange of information to make the interests of the people known, and the application of rewards and punishments from below to make the decision makers accountable. Rewards include reelection, financial support, supportive demonstrations, good opinions in polls, and cooperation with projects.

Punishments are often considered the hallmark of democratic government.[17] The argument goes that even if "the people" cannot practically rule directly, their ability to punish—including remove from office—the legislators and policy makers creates a counterbalance to the power that decision makers have in their control of the state apparatus.[18] Sanctioning options vary widely. Elections are raised to an ideal because they seem to provide the best chance for a peaceful but effective transfer of power, however expensive they might be. But there are many other methods of punishing decision makers: undercutting them by shaming; destroying their reputations; carrying out personal, group, or mass confrontations; exposing their personal foibles; and weakening their ability to communicate. Judicial and quasi-judicial procedures are common. Character assassination or its threat can sometimes be as effective as elections, and physical assassination or its threat—however much we like to believe that we have progressed beyond such violence—is part of the picture. The threat to use any of these methods is often the most effective way of holding decision makers to their task—although, of course, such steps can be misused, weakening as well as promoting representation.

In summary, to identify the institutions that have to be reformed in order to make a political system a representative democracy, we must look to the institutions that shape patterns of decision making, the processes that identify "the people" and link them to the system, and the two-way flow of information and mechanisms of rewards and punishments that ground accountability.

CONVENTIONAL MODELS OF REPRESENTATIVE INSTITUTIONS

What are the institutions that shape the interests of the people, the choices of decision makers, and the flow of information, rewards, and punishment between them? The answers that most people, specialists and nonspecialists alike, give to the question of identifying the institutions do not derive from the kind of general analysis being made here. Rather, they focus on the set of institutions that have come down to us from their beginnings in the seventeenth- and eighteenth-century European liberal revolutions: elections, legislatures, party systems, varied sets of interest groups, and legislative–executive relations.

Those institutions were solutions to historically specific circumstances. They were built for the nation-state, which came to dominate Europe. They expressed the notion of popular sovereignty in the face of the arrogation of power by an individual, a group, or a class. Not only should the welfare of the people be paramount (an old concept), but the people should rule—if not directly, then through their representatives in "assemblies" of the people. Sovereignty further became identified with law giving, and popular sovereignty thus came to be thought of as the people's control of the legislature.[19] The set of people who took on this sovereignty were the citizens. The ancient practice of elections became the favored instrument for holding representatives accountable.

Over the years, many changes took place in the institutions. I will dramatically simplify their evolution by characterizing five models that, roughly speaking, added to or partially replaced one another through time. I believe that these models order most thinking about the institutions of representative democracy (and distract us from important facts that must be addressed). I refer to these models as the deputy model, the partisan model, and three versions of the pluralist model: the corporatist, interest group, and social movement.[20]

• The *deputy model* is related to the origins of the institutions of representative democracy and is based on the notion of representation as essentially the selection of individuals from among components of the society, such as territorial units or corporate entities. These deputies move to some central place and act as delegates of the people who sent them. This is the model emphasized by the influential eighteenth- and nineteenth-century constitutions, and it lies at the core of liberal representative democracy.

At the center of the deputy model is a group of elites elected by constituencies. The communication between representatives and constituents may be infrequent, based on the implicit trust that the people have in their chosen representative as someone knowledgeable about the affairs of the country who does not need constant updating.[21] More commonly now, it involves intense interaction. Since the deputies come from their communities in theory, communication between the "principals" and their "agents" is direct, often informal, and reinforced and strengthened by regular meetings, the press, and, latterly, polls. The two-way communication is intensified by elections, which also serve as the primary sanction to ensure accountability. Parliamentary committees, debates, and voting constitute the central integrating process of decision making: resolving conflicts and enabling collective approaches to major problems. In the deputy model, the institutions that govern are found in constitutions, established legislative procedures, and informal rules and norms that govern the relations between deputies and their constituents. The study of these institutions is, of course, a major preoccupation of political science.

• The *partisan model* is based on political parties, which emerged from factions at royal courts and among followers of prominent leaders or clubs in legislatures and then spread into society. Alongside the functions of organizing elections and legislatures, parties and party systems are a separate channel for "pre-processing" interests around programmatic principles or goals, establishing the agenda for the conflicts of policy and legislation. In some countries, this pre-processing may be carried out in churches and religious communities that are organized around strong sets of politically relevant beliefs. Communication between decision makers and individuals, groups, and communities is, in varying degrees, organized and influenced by the parties, and the differences in their structure and style—from tightly disciplined membership organizations to loose associations of individuals—constitute a major institutional variable that shapes representation. The pattern of interactions between parties—that is, the party system—also is a major organizer of the integrative process that shapes the links in cabinets, in legislatures, and between legislatures and executives, as well as in the media or on the streets. Elections remain the main mechanisms for applying sanctions to enforce accountability, but loss of support or of access to decision centers may take other forms, as well.

In much of the twentieth century, even though their institutionalization was often partial and informal, party systems were felt to be the most important way of identifying "the people" and their desires, choosing legislative representatives, and organizing political communication around programs, identities, and ideologies. Their importance was magnified in times of conflict because of how they came to embody the parties to the conflict and how they dealt (or failed to deal) with ideological and moral differences.

The next three models are pluralist, suggesting a multiplicity of groups being represented in the political process.

• In the *corporatist model*, government incorporates groups directly into its decision-making structures. Historically, these were such "corporations" as religious institutions, guilds, and trading companies. In the early twentieth century, another form evolved (in part consciously anti-socialist) in which groups or class organizations like labor unions, business owners, and commercial interests were formally created or recognized and given a party-like role in legislatures or special corporatist assemblies. In the post–World War II period, there was considerable discussion about neo-corporatism involving an increasingly complex set of groups integrated into government boards and standard-setting agencies.[22] When the ties between government and these corporatist groups are complex, the model shades off into the interest-group version.

• The *interest-group model* sees a multiplicity of interest groups existing independently of the state, but with the intention of shaping policy and law. The people being represented divide into clusters of individuals who share an interest, and organizations are formed to promote it. The interactions between the people and the decision makers is not mediated by acting through official corporatist bodies, but by lobbying, conducting hearings, organizing personal networks of influence, and undertaking public campaigns to sway legislation and policy. The flow of information is much more complex and flexible than in the other models. The integration of conflicting preferences to make policy takes place in the legislature, preceded by public and "backstage" discussions.

• Yet another version of pluralism, the *social-movement model*, shares with the other pluralist models the notion of multiple clusters of interests. But building on the revolutionary partisan tradition, it calls attention to the fundamental dissatisfaction of some groups with the status quo. Those who see no clear path to a politics-as-usual solution to social problems may include religious, racial, and ethnic minorities; immigrants; marginalized workers in times of economic transition; and young people with a view of the good society different from that of the Establishment. Advocates of these and other groups can be ambivalent about the virtues or dangers of being integrated into the system in the manner of corporatist and interest groups. In this model, involvement with formal politics is ordered around challenges to the dominant groups that are in control of the government.

Seeing the social-movement variant as a model of representative democracy assumes (which may well be true) that there are in any society a group of people who are sufficiently opposed to the current arrangements to refuse to play an institutionalized role as a party or an interest group, but whose willingness to confront the political system is not unlimited. Although they may use revolutionary imagery, they are not set on total transformation, only those aspects of society that bear on their "issue." What emerges is a two-level (or more) pattern in which politics takes place—the decision making and the links—but in a different form for the Establishment and the social-movement groups, whose links with decision makers are contentious.[23]

Taken together, these five models—the deputy, partisan, corporatist, interest group, and social movement—provide a rich field for identifying, establishing, monitoring, and reforming the institutions of representation. No doubt, reforming elections (pointed to by the deputy model), forming more responsible political parties (suggested by the partisan model), and passing better laws to govern the influence of interest groups (highlighted by the pluralist models) would offer help in dealing with the problems.

But however influential in guiding our efforts to reform democracy, these models do not capture many sorts of political actions that are crucial to representative democracy. They have become so familiar that they seem almost natural. But they all make crucial and often false assumptions—about the nature of the people, about the structure of the process of legislation and policy making, and about the unity of the process—many of which are false. The six facts about politics that I discuss in the rest of the book upset the assumptions on which these models are based and set a challenge for us to rethink the institutions of representative democracy.

PART II

THE PEOPLE

2

WHICH "PEOPLE"
ARE REPRESENTED IN A
REPRESENTATIVE
DEMOCRACY?

W hen a major company headquartered in one country does business in another country, what is the status of that firm in the "host" country's political system? When legal but noncitizen migrants play a major role in a school system, what is their status in a democracy? When an army from one country is greeted as a force for positive social or political change in another country, what democratically relevant role does it play in the operation of the latter country's political system? When the actions of an international financial institution are very important for the business health of major industries in a country, what status does that financial institution have in the decision making about economic regulation in the country?

The first two sets of facts that pose problems for reforming the institutions of democracy concern the proliferation of actors like these, which have an unclear relation to the political decision-making process. Their activities are often regulated by law and are considered normal or understandable, but whether they constitute "people" who should be represented in the political system is contested, unclear, or simply ignored. Representative democracy is a system "of the people, by the people, and for the people." But who are the people?

The people were declared the beneficiaries of the democratic revolutions two centuries ago that established the basic outlines of modern representative political systems. It was the people that were to be freed from the arbitrary and self-interested rule of the aristocrats, the privileged, the elites.[1] Perhaps as a result, one common meaning of "the people" is the "common people"—the people as not the privileged. The rhetorical popularity of this negative definition of "the people," as in the phrase "a man of the people," continues, implying someone who identifies with those who do not enjoy wealth or privilege. In classic Greek definitions of "democracy," the actors in power were the non-privileged, and a frequent implication was that a government was democratic insofar as it served the interests of the non-privileged.

Although questions about the distribution of benefits still remain crucial—particularly for remedying inequality—questions about the institutions of democracy have tended to turn away from an emphasis on providing for the welfare of the popular class over that of the privileged class, to an emphasis on bringing about equality between them, at least equality before the law and equality of opportunity. The norm for democracy now is somehow to benefit "all the people." And for a specification of who "the people" are, common answers are the whole population of a nation, a territory, or a community, and all those who share a cultural identity.

Notice that in this line of thought, whether speaking of the underprivileged or "everyone," "the people" are identified as those whom the system is meant to benefit. This is a standard definition and is crucial when adopting the criterion I have for evaluating the level of democracy: whether the system serves the people. Representing the people in this sense means that the decision makers act in the interest of the people. There have been many discussions about the best way to specify the members of this group, but rather than trying to resolve the differences, I wish to contrast this approach to conceptualizing "the people" with another.

The other approach starts by asking not who benefits, but whose cooperation, compliance, and acceptance of a decision's legitimacy are required. Who are the people who have a stake in a decision and who, if they oppose it, would make it unworkable? The answer may seem obvious. Most assume that it is the same people: those for whom the system acts are those who will be affected by a decision and will have to accept it. It seems to be almost a definition of democracy that they should be the same.

But these two sets of "people," however much they overlap, are determined by fundamentally different methods and thus are possibly different from each other. And I will argue that they are, in fact, very different, posing dramatic problems for democratic reform. The designation of the "core citizenry," whom the system is supposed to benefit, is a political act—intended or not, explicit or not. Specifying the main beneficiaries of a system means establishing a priority that guides decisions. During the period of state formation and attendant nationalism, the choice to create an "imagined community" as a nation was a key element of the dominance of the nation-state.[2] It is (or should be) a contentious political act to specify such a core set of people because it is an argument that for a specific set of decision makers, one group of people in the world takes precedence among all the people in the world. The contrast is no longer with the privileged, but with the people of other countries (and those within the country who are not citizens). It is a political choice of the most serious kind.[3]

The identity of the people who are linked to the decision-making process because they are affected by the decisions and whose cooperation or compliance is thus required, however, is determined not by a political act, but by the facts. The core citizens are one element of this set of people, but not all of it. This larger set of "people" are important in determining the outcomes of a decision, since they have strong interests and their acceptance of the legitimacy of a policy or a law is important to its effectiveness, which conditions the ability of a government to serve the interests of the core citizens. And the nature of the involvement of all those affected by the decision-making process may have a strong effect on the justice of the decisions for the core citizens as well. All of those affected have a stake in the outcomes of the policy. They are likely to act in defense of that stake. That is what makes the representation of all those affected necessary. They are stakeholders in the outcome and thus will shape its consequences.[4]

The two methods for determining "the people" relevant to representative institutions identifies different sets of people to be linked to the decision-making process. To avoid confusion, I will call them by different names. The group of people whose welfare is prioritized in a democratic system I will call the "core citizenry." Those who are affected I will call the "stakeholders." The special group that requires the attention of reformers are those stakeholders who are not members of the core citizenry. I will call them "quasi-citizens."

Another way to emphasize the distinction between the two ways of determining "the people" is to suggest that two meanings of the word "representation" are involved. One is to promote someone's welfare. The other is to consider someone's interests. If it were true that promoting the welfare of the core citizenry only involves direct links between the decision makers and the core citizenry, while taking into account the interests of the quasi-citizens does not require such links, we might conclude that the institutions of representation concern only the core. But that is manifestly false. Being able to understand the needs, likely reactions, and changing interests of both sets of people requires continual interaction and communication between the decision makers and both the core citizenry and the quasi-citizens—all the stakeholders. Both groups have to be represented in the system in the sense that their interests are tightly involved in the outcomes of a decision, even when the priority given in the decision is consistently, even dramatically, toward the core citizens.[5]

Two facts about these two sets of people make them important for thinking about democratic reform. First, the quasi-citizens may be a large and influential group whose links to the system, their representation, have to be similar, if not identical, to those of the core citizens (as discussed in chapters 3 and 4). Second, different groups of quasi-citizens are affected by different decisions, whereas the core citizenry may remain relatively constant. Stakeholders vary by issue, since the stakes vary according to the problem at hand. This is only one reason for concluding that the structure of representation is constantly changing (and we return to it at several points, especially in chapter 10), but the consequences are particularly important when we consider quasi-citizens.

Both core and quasi-citizens change, but at very different rates. Those who are accepted as the core citizenry have quite fuzzy and sometimes contested boundaries, but, barring revolution or secession, changes among them are likely to be relatively rare and gradual. Quasi-citizens are likely to vary from issue to issue and be—even when they are in normal and familiar relationships—in frequently changing networks that spread out from the government that is making the decisions. If, as I argue, the representation of quasi-citizens is necessary for making law and policy in the interest of the core citizenry, the institutions that may ensure such representation do not resemble those in the five conventional models discussed in chapter 1, all of which basically assume a stable set of institutions representing a stable set of citizens.

In a small town, for example, problems demanding political action would include collecting and recycling trash, agreeing on the use of publicly owned land, educating children, and dealing with delinquent young people. For each issue, the process of making a decision and taking action on the part of the community government affects a specific collection of people (and thus stakeholders), and this set of people will vary from issue to issue. A particular set of stakeholders will come together to tackle each problem, working their way through (or not) differences in goals and methods, deciding on a common approach, finding the resources to deal with it, and establishing the ways to implement a solution or a compromise. And each decision network involves the local government and some range of its core citizens, but many others who are not.

Dealing with delinquent young people probably would engage the active participation of parents in the town and local medical professionals, but also would involve the storeowners in other towns subject to shoplifting or vandalism and the young girls or boys subject to unwanted approaches at regional schools. It would also include state officials, law-enforcement personnel, and state educational authorities. The town government might, in fact, simply give up and let parents and outsiders handle the problem. But many towns might seek to establish local work and charitable programs for teens, workshops to promote home security, or sports programs to address the needs of potential "delinquents." Local decision makers, in order to serve the people of their community, their core citizenry, would have to build extensive lines of information exchange with many authorities and individuals in other jurisdictions.

A different set of people would be involved making decisions about collecting and recycling trash. The decisions about trash collection (at least in my town) would have an impact on the receiving sites in other communities, supervising officials in superior jurisdictions responsible for recycling and environmental questions, workmen who come from other jurisdictions to build houses in town, and many others. Even if the interests of the town's core citizenry were given priority in the decisions made, the process would have to discover the interests and likely reactions of the citizens of the towns that receive the trash and the state officials who are responsible for recycling.

And the difference between core and quasi-citizens would no doubt grow as we move to more complex political systems.

I am not pointing to the obvious fact that different sets of individuals in and out of the town would become actively engaged in the decision-making process. Whether they become active or not, the stakeholders—including quasi-citizens—must be recognized and represented. Decisions made on school policy without an awareness of the likely reactions of taxpayers in the town, even if they do not participate (perhaps because they have no children in school), would risk rejection of the budget at the town meeting. Decisions made on school policy about religious observance without an awareness of the possible reactions of the courts or religious authorities would be foolish.

That sets of individuals making up the relevant "people" shift from issue to issue, even if the government remains the same, is not a conventional formulation. It is much more common to assume that there is one people, a single set of individuals, and all questions about participation and benefits and costs are shared by all. And, to be sure, this way of conceptualizing the "people" has some uses in reinforcing solidarity and mutual obligation. In my local example, one speaks of "the community," which shares everything. At another level, one speaks of "the nation." That it should be considered as a single unit is even treated as a moral imperative. Everyone in the community or nation "ought" to feel that he or she is affected as much as everyone else. That is manifestly not true about almost every decision, but it does urge members of the community to care about others.

But if we turn from exhortatory rhetoric to analysis—and reform—of political processes, it is an important and costly conceptual mistake to consider the sets of people involved in making decisions about different issues to be a single unit. It is a mistake, perhaps undertaken to make the task of institutional reform easier, to consider a single set of procedures as the means to deal with various issues and their different stakeholders. A common practice is to think of a city council and a mayor as the unit responsible for all decision making in a local government, and the methods of discovering preferences, predicting likely reactions, weighing alternatives, bargaining, and deliberating as wrapped up in the informal personal connections that the council members and the mayor have with all stakeholders, with accountability handled by periodic elections.

This simplification distorts our understanding of the process and the institutions that guide it—and therefore what has to be reformed. Even at the level of local government, patterns emerge of establishing committees to make recommendations, holding open meetings, and using media to cover one or another aspect of the process. Rules and customs and habits regulate these sometimes "informal" practices. Those should be the subject of reform. And obviously at the level where the issues are broader—say, at the national level—the pattern is much more complex.

Including people in the institutions of representative government on the basis of their stake in the policies and laws that the government produces has an important impact on our understanding of those institutions. The norm adopted may be rules for reaching out to various groups, or the variability may be left to an all-purpose legislature to handle, but some attention has to be given to the problem. And since the variability is not a commonly identified problem of representative government, we have to reconceptualize the institutions. The identity of quasi-citizens changes constantly, issue by issue. We have to regard democratic institutions as the regulators of a dynamic system.

3

QUASI-CITIZENS IN THE COMMUNITY ARE REPRESENTED

Knowing and acting on the preferences of and information from many noncitizens within the territory are necessary for making just and effective decisions.

Fact 1

The presence of "others" has always been part of human society. Families and communities and ethnic groups found strangers in their midst—sometimes with pleasure, sometimes with hostility, often welcomed for their usefulness or sometimes merely tolerated. Sometimes they were servants; sometimes, masters. Sometimes their presence had a specific purpose; sometimes it was due to the accidents of geography.

Unless they have specially arranged immunity, people who cross borders are subject to the laws of the host country. But it is not so easy to specify what happens to a person's right to be heard in lawmaking when he or she crosses a border. A large group of such people have stakes in the operations of their host countries, seek to influence what is decided, and thus become quasi-citizens.[1]

A foreigner who spends a week touring a country is not given the right to vote. To earn that right takes more time and more significant commitment. Some might say that those who wish to influence outcomes should take the time and effort to become "naturalized" citizens. But there have always been people who have not wanted to change their citizenship or who are not eligible for citizenship, but who are important to and form part of the community within the boundaries of the host nation.

Because of the importance of noncitizens, there have been numerous experiments in giving them the vote, usually in some limited way, such as only for local elections.[2] Because of the limited nature of these experiments, it would appear that quasi-citizens have to settle for obeying laws that they have no share of responsibility for making.

But the right to vote is not the only sign of participation and representation in a system. The fact is that a large number of people are recognized by decision makers, who take into account their preferences and seek their cooperation and compliance. I call them "quasi-citizens" because they have some, but not all, of the characteristic of citizens, and they do participate in political processes. They do not identify with the local community or the nation (although a few may wish to be accepted at some point). They are not-Germans living and working in Germany or not-Chinese living and working in China. That they do not vote is a fact, and in some few cases that may be important.

There are many signs of institutions—norms, practices, laws—that link them to the political process. Over time, many quasi-citizens acquire roles with labels that imply a status in law or convention. Official representatives of other sovereigns are diplomats. Some of the people who come to work are guest workers or undocumented. People who buy and sell goods are foreign traders. People who build or finance industries are foreign investors. Troops of a foreign intervening army are occupiers or peacekeepers. People who want to join the nation are immigrants, and those who seek protection from oppression at home are refugees. People who come to enjoy the country are tourists and perhaps become expatriates. Cultural workers are visiting writers, painters, and composers in residence. Dancers, musicians, and actors are touring performers. Representatives of international health organizations, members of charitable groups, and officials of microcredit banks are aid workers. Smugglers, drug dealers, and sex traffickers are international criminals. Each label suggests not only these people's occupations, but the ways in which they are tied to decision making. Together, they are, to define them negatively, noncitizens or aliens, many of whom are nevertheless engaged in the political process.[3]

That engagement may be brief, such as a military intervention with a narrow achievable goal, although, as we know, that may turn into an extended mission or an occupation. It could be a short-term exploration for natural resources that fails or turns into a long-term investment. An attempt to introduce a new product into local markets may end with withdrawal or sale of assets to a local company, but it may become a regular trading relationship. Even in short episodes, they may connect with politics. But when they are of longer duration, complex involvements in politics are likely to develop.

The varying, but time-delimited, quality of the interaction with politics may seem to distinguish this involvement from that of the core citizenry. But if we are thinking about political decision making and not the symbolic identification with the nation or community, the issue-specific quality of the participation by these quasi-citizens in "normal politics" suggests that the involvement is not so different from that of core citizens. And, indeed, diplomatic representatives or foreign companies with a major investment—say, in a mine—way well be much more attentive to the political process than the distractible core citizens.

The interests of those who do become involved are intertwined with the legislative and policy decisions being made, and it is in the interests of the core citizenry that they do so. In fact, of course, these foreign quasi-citizens may be ignored or rejected, and members of the core citizenry may do their best to expel them. But as long as they retain a significant stake in the country, they are part of the process. They have influence and are represented in most political systems, although usually irregularly and without the same attention to principles governing fair representation as are, at least nominally, applied to core citizens.

The relationships of in-community quasi-citizens to the state, its laws, and its political institutions take many forms. Some have a very formal relationship, linked to their status in their home nations or in international organizations. They include diplomatic representatives, consular officials, members of military missions, official cultural and travel representatives, members of trade missions, development workers, and employees of the United Nations or other international organizations. Many with working links in business, educational, or cultural institutions have a formal status given by a visa or some form of work or residence permit. Foreign investors, traders, and employees of foreign and domestic companies are often tightly linked to relevant lobbying groups. Foreign-based philanthropic or development agencies may have contracts or understandings with local or national governments. Expatriate retirees may play an informal or a formal role in local communities. Some have a formalized temporary status, such as students, visiting professors, and guest workers. Some without formal status, such as illegal migrants, are mostly law-abiding members of society integrated into communities economically with support networks among themselves. Some are in tension with the law, but tightly integrated into underground mafia-like arrangements, such as drug dealers and arms traffickers, with possible understandings with local authorities.

These people are subject to the laws of the host countries in which they live and work. Most pay taxes; contribute capital, skills, or labor to the economy; send their children to school; use health-care facilities and public-transport systems; write books; and teach. Some exploit workers, extract resources, clog highways, receive welfare, and give (or extract) bribes.

What of their political role? The question sounds odd because in almost all countries, foreigners are excluded from participating in politics. But this shows more about the use of the word "politics" than anything about the role of noncitizens in the process of decision making. The diplomatic representative of a powerful neighboring state may rigorously avoid the appearance of intervening in politics, but can exercise great influence in the shaping of trade or security policy. A nongovernmental organization may disavow any intention of involving itself in politics, but presses hard for a government effort to change health conditions for children. Foreign tourist organizations may lobby for concessions on tourist visas and construction in resort areas. They all are striving to shape decisions. The question is not whether these quasi-citizens should be represented. They are represented. Whether for the benefit of the core citizenry or not is a question at least in part decided by the norms, laws, and practices—that is, the institutions—that are in place to regulate the links between the quasi-citizens and the decision makers.

In different ways, most of these groups of quasi-citizens must be and are built into the system in some fashion. They fit awkwardly into the models of representation discussed in chapter 1, so perceiving, let alone prescribing, the institutions in the usual sense—to promote effectiveness and justice— is difficult. Although the channels are not "normal," the influences of these groups are shaped by various norms and laws and arrangements. In other words, there are institutions that shape their representation, for good or ill. An extreme nationalist position might be that no representation of noncitizens is better than any at all, so the dominant institution would be negative:

prohibition. But far more rational would be an effort to regulate the links, even if it was done exclusively for the benefit of the core citizenry.

Two examples of such noncitizens may make the direction of the argument clearer. I will briefly discuss foreign investors and illegal migrants.

The presence of foreign investors has long been a contentious issue, especially in less-developed countries. Questions turn on whether they enhance or detract from national development, whether they gain too much advantage or bring too little benefit, or whether they import noxious cultural influences or welcome "modernization." Some of the more radical anti-imperialist doctrines seem to imply that the world—or at least some particular nation—would be better without such investment. But in the current "globalized" environment, the questions have turned to how best to attract and regulate foreign investors, not banish them. Even for the most negative, the question has shifted from whether foreigners should be welcomed to how they should be treated—keeping in mind issues of justice, cultural influences, health, and the environment, on the one hand, and growth, new technology, and productivity on the other.

Much is at stake for the investors, of course: the conditions of operating, the threats of the loss of their property through nationalization, the access to labor and markets, and a whole host of factors affecting rates of profit and their way of life. The people of the country in which they are investing obviously have much at stake, too. Rates of growth, patterns of inequality, and health of the environment may turn heavily on the manner in which the foreign investors participate in the system. Other stakeholders in the country are concerned: labor unions, potential competitors, and those with principled positions on economic integration and global warming.

These choices are the stuff of policy making in almost all countries. Some might argue that many of these interactions ought to be left to the market and kept out of politics, but the reality is that the policies of the so-called host government are important to both the foreign investor and the core citizenry, and these policies are set through political means. From both sides, foreign and domestic, there is a strong incentive to connect all investors with the political process, and that they are not citizens is immaterial. The goal of getting them involved is not based on their rights (although in some cases, developing international law may provide that, too), but on the mutual advantage, the desire to secure cooperation, and the need to articulate solutions to ongoing, recurring, and new problems. This is precisely the situation where representative mechanisms and the institutions to regulate them come into play.

Representing noncitizens in the political process in order to make decisions in the interests of the core citizenry may seem to be a strange idea, but I think there are several reasons for believing that this is the way to think about it. The kind of representative system we are looking for makes decisions for the welfare of the core citizenry of a community. These decisions are based on information about the actors and the likely consequences of possible actions. The participation of foreign investors in a serious way is not only possible, but necessary. They are engaged in the polity, the decision-making processes. They are part of "the people," even though in judging the outcomes, these quasi-citizens are subordinate to the core citizenry.

In what becomes a repeated theme in looking at representation, the development of knowledge through the links between decision makers and foreign investors is important. Framing economic policy requires that decision makers try to predict whether certain incentives will lead to more investment, whether certain imports or distribution schemes will make a business more or less successful, whether certain financial groups will stay the course to provide support, and hundreds of other facts about the situation. It is possible that the decision makers have the information (or believe that they do) necessary for making such calculations, and they may think that a few experts on the topic from within their team can supply any deficiencies. But in another consistent theme that emerges in these pages, it is often better to listen to the people—in this case, the foreign investors.

Lobbyists and members of the management of foreign concerns can provide information that often is not available elsewhere. With rapidly changing conditions, the danger of using outdated or stereotyped information is serious. An expert in an ivory tower or an employee of a government minister may well provide out-of-date or biased information. Information from people engaged directly with a problem is crucial. That it must be confronted with other points of view is important, too, for making not only intelligent decisions, but also just ones. That the information about the potential decisions affecting foreign investors may be accurate or distorted or wrong, that it may be provided merely to enhance the success of a foreign investor or developed by its rivals or enemies to limit its success, points to the need for regulation and standards—formal or informal—to ensure the quality of the information. But it does not obviate the fact that some mechanism for making the interests of foreign investors a part of the decision-making process—in other words, representing them—is necessary.

Making policy also requires some reasonable guarantee of compliance. Foreign investors have incentives to cheat or evade, as does any business concern. Compliance is always a problem. Foreign investors are, on the one hand, usually more exposed to enforcement actions, perhaps because they are less likely than domestic firms to have personal ties to the apparatus of government, and therefore evasion of regulations may be more dangerous. On the other hand, they have a more realistic opportunity than citizens to simply withdraw from a country. Depending on the amount of fixed capital and other links they have in the host country, they may simply invest in another market. But foreign investors, like other groups, often choose "voice" over "exit," attempting to shape policy rather than leave a country.[4]

From the standpoint of the political system, it is possible to secure compliance with policies and laws through heavy financial penalties, taxes, limitations on access to markets, and the like. But raising costs can go only so far, and some way to reassure foreign investors that they will be listened to and taken seriously is almost always a part of the strategy. Some means of conveying information, sanctions, and commitments is inevitable. In other words, if any foreign investors are perceived as having important roles to play in the economy, there will be some mechanism for making them a part of the community—that is, of representing them in the political system. If they are of any significant size, the choice is not *whether* they will be represented in the political system, but *how* they will be, and whether the system integrates their preferences and information in a way that serves the interests of the core citizenry and the whole community.

While I have been lumping together "foreign investors," it is clear that multinational oil companies, Asian suppliers of manufactured goods, European banks and fashion-design companies, oil-rich Arab businessmen, and computer-tablet manufacturers have very different interests, pose very different challenges, and use different means to try to influence government policies. Whether they are brought under some general facility in the government, such as the Ministry of Foreign Affairs or an international trade agency, the manner in which they interact with decision makers will vary by issue and circumstances. An oil company headquartered in one country that is seeking rights to drill in another country's territorial waters will work with or on the officials who are responsible for the ecological health of the region; the authorities that deal with fishing regulations and coastal security; and the refineries, distributors, and legislators from the relevant states. The legislative process, with its committee hearings, may play a lesser role. Executive commissions may be set up. The decision network that will become involved in the final policy decision will, to some extent, be tailor-made to tackle this issue.

Two aspects of the processes that link the foreign investors with the political system stand out. First, they are unlikely to be embedded in the usual constitutionally based representative institutions; rather, they are much more likely to be channeled through administrative agencies or through informal, sometimes secretive ties or sometimes high-profile media-covered talks with decision makers. Second, they are likely to vary greatly from sector to sector and over time. Meaningful reform requires identifying or creating institutions that find a way to manage the varied and changing patterns that operate outside the classical political institution of parties, elections, and legislatures.

Another group of quasi-citizens—significant in many countries just now—are the migrants who enter a country without documents or who overstay their legally permitted visit as visitors, students, refugees, and the like. The most discussed recently are those who are drawn by opportunities to earn more than they could at home and by the promise of either future regularization or tolerable freedom to work without official permission and return home with what they earn. Illegal migrants become significant whenever some countries experience economic expansion not shared by others. The particular needs and desires of groups of such migrants depend on many factors, including access to transportation that makes entry and occasional return plausible, their personal networks, and the conditions of their employment.

The most common way that these illegal workers relate to the political process is as a policy problem. What to do with them? Send them home as lawbreakers? Make it possible for some of them to become citizens or guest workers? Welcome them as an economic resource? Defend them as human beings endowed with rights? The choices that are made will affect not only the migrants themselves, but the core citizenry, since migrants compete for jobs, provide needed services, create ethnic tensions, may offer examples of strong family behavior, may harbor criminals, and may offer examples of cultural diversity important for the education of core citizens. The rhetoric that suggests their effects as all negative or all positive are clearly just that— rhetoric. Whatever priorities are set for the core citizens, the problem is the same as before: how to take the illegal migrants into account in the political process in a way that will produce the best results.

Policy decisions must be based on a great deal of information about the migrants. Does the fact that they entered the country illegally or overstayed their visit mean that they are more or less likely to commit other kinds of crimes and under what conditions? Will they facilitate the growth of drug gangs or be drawn to the claims of terrorists? Conversely, will they join the fight against drug trafficking or terrorism? What sorts of work will they take, and are they competing for those jobs with other workers? What variations in skills and training do they have, and what sorts of opportunities would they take to improve them? Are they likely to be healthy or sick and, therefore, a drain on health-care facilities? Do they perform well in school, or is illiteracy and the language barrier insuperable? How effective are traditional, family-, or community-based educational or health services? What influences their assimilation into local culture or accentuates their desire to live in areas with other people of the same heritage? Are they able to live in a multicultural society, and what are their perceptions about the attitudes and actions of the local culture to them? What kind of reaction do they typically have to discrimination based on cultural differences, economic competition, or criminal behavior, real or imagined?

Policies on the admission of migrants into the country and their expulsion, assimilation, or control are, or should be, based on answers to these sorts of questions. In the likely case that mass deportation is impossible or undesirable, policies require information, and, as argued in relation to foreign investors, that means establishing information links between decision makers and the migrants. Decisions about investing in roads, water systems, and sanitation in their communities; about deploying police; about building and equipping schools; about providing health care; and about managing common resources like parks and highways require answers to these questions, too. Efforts to promote investment in certain areas will require knowing whether workers will be there; what training they will need; what they, as consumers, will buy; and so on. Very specific kinds of information about the illegal migrants will be essential to rational decision making, even when there is an explicit determination that "natives" will receive preferential treatment. Knowing "how much the migrants can take" and what discriminatory actions against them will cost in terms of, say, law enforcement, lost labor, or even plain civility of life are required for making rational decisions. And if, as in many traditions, some measure of comity and respect for human beings is a priority, the need for accurate, continually updated information is even greater.

Decision makers have to know what the migrants want as well, not necessarily because they choose to satisfy those demands, but because they need the compliance of migrants with basic laws establishing order on the streets, acceptable behavior in schools, participation in or at least acceptance of community projects, and many other aspects of social life. Representation may have its central purpose in "making the people sovereign," but a significant reason for paying attention to the preferences of people is to integrate them into a functioning whole, to achieve a working society.

How do decision makers discover these needs and propensities, these desires and perspectives? Illegal migrants seem about as far away from participating in the normal political process of shaping policy as one might imagine. They are not represented through the political mechanisms available to citizens, embedded in the conventional models of representation: they do not vote and thus are unlikely to be courted by political parties. The frequent differences in language, culture, and ethnicity between newcomers and natives increase barriers to simple communication. Although various forms of organizations and social movements may link with them, they are unlikely to have a regular legal, recognized lobbying organization, as in the interest-group model. Despite all these barriers, however, it is crucial that they be linked to decision making.

So where does the information needed by decision makers come from? Academic experts, government agents, local police, community groups, investigative reporters, charitable organizations, and human rights activists provide some information, although it is likely to be selective and erratically sought and sometimes tendentious. That the process of information gathering and policy integration often takes place with little participation from the illegal migrants themselves does not necessarily mean that the laws and policies will be less good than those for citizens; after all, most debates and discussions take place and most decrees are issued without much participation from the affected groups. But changes happen so quickly that success in making decisions without regular, personal communication is very unlikely. Without it, the information about the migrants' preferences, likely reactions, needs, and likelihood of compliance is erratic, imperfect, subject to stereotypes and manipulation, and a recipe for failure.

The need to create links between decision makers and illegal migrants draws attention to the norms and procedures, the laws and understandings that shape who gets to speak for these migrants and what principles are followed in presenting the information about them, discussing it, and coming to conclusions. Again, as with foreign investors, the processes of representation are likely to take place outside conventional representative institutions and are highly variable. The challenge is to develop institutions to shape these processes in order to make policies and laws effective and just.

Taking into account illegal migrants or any non-nationals, even though it requires that their interests be seriously considered, does not always mean promoting their interests. It is possible that the way in which the interests of noncitizens are taken into account is to oust them—for example, to carry out the often threatened repatriation of illegal immigrants. Whether that is good for the core citizenry depends on circumstances. It is possible that, say, expelling all illegal migrants in the United States would be good for both American citizens, forcing them to find alternatives for cheap labor, and Mexican migrants, saving them from a violent backlash in the United States and pushing the Mexican government to adopt policies that would make emigration unprofitable. Although I am strongly inclined to argue that other alternatives—such as allowing illegal migrants to stay in the United States—would benefit both the migrants and the core citizens, my point is that any policy necessarily involves representing the migrants.

Standing back from the examples of foreign investors and illegal migrants and considering all in-country quasi-citizens and politics, there are two conclusions to be drawn.

• These quasi-citizens are engaged meaningfully with the policy process, and thus they are, willy-nilly, part of "the people" being represented. They are a significant set of individuals, groups, and communities that are closely enough tied to the society in which they live that policy decisions have to take them into account.

• "Taking them into account" means more than just knowing their preferences and situations. It almost always involves consciously accommodating their interests in the final outcome. What is at stake is not just being "clever" and strategic vis-à-vis quasi-citizens, but finding a solution that deals with them as well as with the core citizens. Quasi-citizens may have major resources (military representatives of a powerful neighbor, international business consortia) or be individually and collectively weak (illegal migrants, expatriate communities). They may profess to be disinterested in politics (development missions, international health commissions) or frankly self-interested (commodities buyers, foreign students training for jobs at home). Making policy or writing laws that deals with such groups means that they are represented, however well or badly.

To repeat, my argument has nothing to do with the relative priority in benefiting the quasi-citizens in comparison with the core citizens. Who and how privileged the core citizenry is to be, as I said earlier, is a political decision. I do believe that because of the ever-increasing intertwining of core citizens with the rest of the world, the rational pursuit of the interests of the core citizens requires that more and more attention be paid to serving the interests of quasi-citizens—indeed, the most convincing definition of "globalization" may be the shrinking ability of a group to rationally raise its own interests far above those of all others. But my point here is merely to say that quasi-citizens are being represented in decision making, and democratic reform requires that the institutions that regulate that process be on the agenda of democratic reform.

What are these institutions, the institutions that do or do not tend to make the representation of quasi-citizens yield effective and just decisions? It is not true that there are no such rules and regulations. Many old and new laws, practices, norms, and permanent procedures are connected with dealing with non-nationals. The elaborate rituals of diplomacy and the regulations that govern the participation of foreign businesses in financing elections are two examples. Whether they are adequate to deal with the two aspects highlighted in this chapter—the importance of activity outside the classic institutions, and the need to adapt to very different actors at different times—is to be doubted. The three areas of institutionalization that I put forward in the conclusion as necessary because of the "facts"—the construction and reconstruction of decision networks relevant to specific problems, the management of information, and the incorporation of actors especially for particular decisions—are very much involved in dealing with quasi-citizens.

Let us turn to the next fact: that decision makers have to represent people and authorities in jurisdictions other than theirs.

4

QUASI-CITIZENS IN OTHER JURISDICTIONS ARE REPRESENTED

Governments often have to establish representative-like linkages with other governments and their citizens.

Fact 2

A political system manages a state and territory that is embedded in a world of other nations, as well as supra- and subnational governments, each with its own core citizenries, decision-making systems, and authoritative decision makers. Much of what any government has to do involves acting in other jurisdictions or deciding on nominally domestic issues that heavily involve people in other jurisdictions. This is a problem for many theories about representative democracy because most of the concepts conventionally used to characterize representative democratic institutions are concerned with the way in which the people give themselves laws, not with bringing other governments and citizens of other countries into the discussion. They implicitly assume that the representatives of the core citizenry charged with foreign policy know enough about others to make policy in the interest of the core.

The relationship between a set of decision makers and the governments and citizens of other polities takes many forms. The first is closest to the types treated in chapter 3, involving decisions about domestic issues in which the governments and people of other countries have a strong influence. The second concerns the citizens and authorities of a subordinate "sovereign" state or province in a federal system. The third involves the government and members of an "autonomous" ethnically based region in a country. The fourth concerns the government and broad citizenry of an international political body (such as the European Union and the United Nations). Finally, the fifth relates to the links between the government and the people of a colony or militarily occupied country.

As an example of the first form, consider Canada's economic interests in the United States. The government and citizens of the United States constitute a major concern for the people and policy makers of Canada. Deciding on the effectiveness of policies to promote trade or foster certain lines of imports and exports depends heavily on the tastes and preferences of American consumers. The policy makers, to make good decisions for Canadians, also must know about and get the cooperation of American manufacturers, transport companies, and other businesses. Even though the priority of the Canadian decision makers is to promote the welfare of Canadian citizens and not the interests of American consumers and businesses, they must learn what Americans want, anticipate what they are likely to do in response to trade incentives or threats, and devise a way to "teach" them what the options are and thus what they "should want." This may involve anything from promotional media to official information sessions with major firms. This "intelligence" is provided through the media, through systematic surveys conducted by private firms for Canadian government agencies, and through travelers, research organizations, or diplomatic missions. And like all such interactions, it is two way. Canadian officials may wish to educate American businesses about opportunities or restrictions, and American companies may make requests or demands for particular goods or special privileges. As for the sanctions of accountability held by the American quasi-citizens, the Canadians may be the target of punishments from American businesses in the form of withholding compliance, shaming in the media, undertaking legal proceedings under treaty obligations or international law, and many other ways in which officials are held accountable. American consumers cannot vote in Canadian elections, but they can influence the credibility and perhaps even the electability of Canadian officeholders. The Canadians may still hold that their primary obligation is to rule in the interest of the Canadian core citizenry, but the American consumers and businesses are a significant quasi-constituency for a specific range of issues.

The relationship is obviously complicated by the fact that the American consumers and businesses are within a political system of their own, managed by the government of the United States. And that government has the power to disrupt or facilitate the economic flows that are at issue. So the representative democratic policy-making system of Canada has to deal with the government of the United States, which means the political system.

In some simplified models, this is a part of "foreign policy," and the recognized links between the systems are reduced to the interaction of the two governments (trade treaties, guarantees of access of goods shipments, and the like). The democratic part of the Canadian system enters into the picture in the form of the accountability of the prime minister, whose Department of Foreign Affairs and International Trade conducts the relations and who is held responsible for the results in a periodic election or votes of confidence. The trade, sales, transportation, and financing of goods are considered part of the market relationship between Canadian and American private individuals and groups, and are regulated by general market "hidden hands," within agreed-on rules by the two governments.

It is obvious, I think, that this overview is grossly oversimplified. The Canadian policy makers clearly have and must rely for many decisions on links with both the American producers and consumers—the quasi-citizens—*and* the government of the United States. Given the closeness of the countries and the explosion of communications links, it would take a major crackdown on information flows to reproduce the conventional model. The problem for democracy is not, *per impossible*, to force information into the hands of the executive, but to promote information that serves justice and effectiveness of policy for the Canadian public. The Canadian policy-making system must have up-to-date, ongoing information about American consumers and producers, knowledge about the state of politics in the United States to decide how and when to lobby for laws and decisions in the American system, and some idea of the prospects for a continuing productive relationship between the two nations.

That the decision makers of Canada need information about the citizens and government of the United States will readily be granted, I suspect. Doesn't it merely mean that Canadian policy makers need good intelligence? Perhaps, but good intelligence in this case (and probably in all cases) is not a matter of hiring an "expert" who knows all these facts or setting up a secret spying service, but establishing the two-way links with the people in question. Knowing the likely reactions of the target people, their preferences, and the limits of their tolerance (of, say, a price rise) is more the sort of trade of information that involves consent-generating, compliance-guaranteeing connection similar to the relationship that the decision makers have with their own constituents than the image of experts or spies.[1] Canadian decision makers hear what American consumers and producers are saying, very often from their own people, since the two economies and cultures are so closely intertwined. Hearing it in such a way that benefits both sides is as much a goal as is what we think of as "normal" representation.

One might imagine cases (and extreme nationalists surely do) in which the interests of the Canadian core citizenry are so profoundly at odds with those of the American consumers, producers, and government that two-way communication is impossible. Such a situation would be parallel to one in which totally alienated factions within either country might not be susceptible to incorporation into a representative democratic scheme. Such breakdowns or stalemates are always possible, but they suggest either a serious pathology or a revolutionary situation. In this case, I do not believe that many would argue that the interests of Canadian decision makers and American consumers and producers are so profoundly at odds that no agreement is possible.

More to the point, the improvement of representative democracy depends on the information linkage of Canadian decision makers with the government and citizens of the United States, and any attention to the reform of the institutions of democratic government will have to pay attention to ways of limiting the possibility for errors, biased information from self-interested parties, excessive deference to perceived elites, and bias against migrants or other minorities.

There are many other examples of the way in which democratic decision makers must reach out and somehow incorporate governments and citizens of other jurisdictions in order to benefit their own core citizenry. Intertwined economies, the focus of this Canada–United States example, are common to all countries, but it is far from the only issue in which quasi-citizenship comes into play. Managing cultural and educational exchanges, regulating migration, controlling terrorism, and fighting sex trafficking would generate conclusions similar to the ones given with regard to the economic relations between Canada and the United States.

Other situations that confound assumptions about representation are those in which a government acts directly in other jurisdictions. When doing so, the decision makers are not, of course, making law. That is done by the decision makers in the other jurisdictions. But that does not make representative institutions irrelevant. Much of what governments do domestically is also not lawmaking. Governments invest in infrastructure, send police to protect particular sets of people, build dams and power plants, and bail out weak banks. These actions may be framed as laws, but they do not take the form of finding formulas that can be enforced as a universal standard for those within the territory; rather, they direct the use of public resources in particular situations. These are policy decisions, in contrast to lawmaking, and usually are lumped together with the decisions of policy makers in domestic politics. But in the case of a government acting in another jurisdiction, the distinct qualities become more relevant because action can be only policy making. It involves the deployment of the resources of the acting country in other jurisdictions. This is true even if the policy is pressing for a law—for example, the adoption or strengthening of the enforcement of universal rights by the United Nations. The decisions of a government, whether backed up with small or great resources, seek either to lobby a different authority or to shape the behavior of people outside that government's jurisdiction, and that creates quasi-citizens.

The most fully and consciously institutionalized such relationships are in federal systems. Such systems vary greatly, but they always involve some division of lawmaking power between the central government and the subordinate jurisdictions (provinces, states). The central government makes decisions about certain issues, and the subordinate jurisdictions, others. In the United States, for example, law enforcement and education are largely under the authority of the states. In theory, for those issues, decision makers in the state political process are linked to the citizens of the states and for issues over which the federal government has the authority, the federal government is linked to the citizens of the country as a whole. There are two nested sets of representative institutions.

In cases of uncertainty of authority due to ambiguity or overlapping jurisdictions, how does the federal government deal with the citizens of the subordinate unit, or the reverse? There is often a high level of institutionalization of these relationships because federal systems are usually written into constitutions and overseen in part by courts. Within changing but usually defined limits, the policies of the national government aimed at influencing the citizens of the provinces or states are subject to careful regulation, with the rules often taking up a significant part of the constitutional document. These institutions regulate when the national government can act within the subunit, and democratic values are preserved (well or badly) by the courts or other means.[2]

But even in highly institutionalized systems, it is clear that the decision-making authority between the central and subordinate jurisdictions is not perfectly regulated, which in itself brings into play the complexities of inter-jurisdictional politics. The states in the United States may decide to act in areas nominally assigned to the federal government—for example, the recent case in which Arizona passed its own law on immigration or, more generally, when a state acts in a foreign country to build markets or attract investment. The state decision makers not only need knowledge about the preferences and likely responses of the people in the foreign country, but must assess the interests of the citizens of the other states in the United States. Whatever the legal assignment of responsibilities, the state policy makers have to work out policies with both the government and the people of the foreign country, as well as the citizens and government of the United States. This is a wide set of quasi-citizens who have no vote on the specific state decision, but on whose acceptance and compliance the success of the policy depends.

Similarly, the decisions made by the central government about laws and policies that are considered state prerogatives—for example, educational policy in the United States—require the federal decision makers to establish links with the state citizens as quasi-citizens. Since the citizens of the states are also citizens of the federal system, this may not appear to be a problem. But since the arrangements on, say, educational policy vary from state to state and have been shaped by the political processes in the states, the federal decision makers have to secure the compliance and acceptance of their policy from what are, in this case, quasi-citizens of the central government.

If the decision makers in the federal government succeed in convincing all the state citizens and decision makers that, in fact, an issue is subject to the authority of the federal government, not the states, then they have won the struggle. More likely and more in need of links to the issue-specific quasi-citizens is a resolution that mandates a continuing division of authority. There is an ongoing discussion about the powers of the super- and subordinate entities, involving an ongoing meshing and re-meshing of the two political systems. Democratic reforms that look only at the traditional models of relationships between the core citizenry and their decision makers are far off the mark.

Other complications arise in the case of autonomous regions based on ethnic differences, especially when there is a history of conflict or oppression between the primary group and the subordinate culture. The intention— rhetorically, at least—in a world of "multiculturalism" is to make it possible for people to live under the moral, legal, and social norms associated with their culture. The leaders (decision makers) in the ethnic enclave have to be close to their own people, but they also must be very involved in assessing the attitudes of those in the larger community. The larger community consists of not just the central government, which is crucial, but the citizens who might or might not accept the autonomy of the enclave, might or might not become involved in trade between the nation and the region, might or might not support the exclusive rights of the members of the enclave to the natural resources in its territory, and many other things. Although the enclave is autonomous in, say, its legal right to make certain kinds of law, it must take into account the preferences, likely responses, and compliance of the people in the nation as a whole. Multiculturalism would rarely go as far as allowing the stoning of adulteresses, but some variations in marriage laws might be welcome. The citizens of the larger community become the quasi-citizens of the decision makers in the enclave. In order to make decisions in the interest of their core constituents, they must establish links with the quasi-citizens. The same sort of analysis could be done for the way that citizens of the enclave become quasi-citizens for the policy makers of the larger system.

A situation parallel to federalism and indigenous enclaves, but reversed, occurs when a nation-state joins an international political organization that has decision-making power. To be sure, the concept of quasi-citizens would not fit well in one common twentieth-century model of such international regimes. In keeping with the emphasis on nation-states, some supranational authorities were established with the proviso that member states retain their sovereignty over all matters and a decision by the supranational body can be made only by the unanimous agreement of all chief executives expressed as treaties signed by all. The issue of representation of policies made by one country was turned rhetorically into a question of "foreign policy." In this model, representation is in the picture only at the moment of parliamentary support for or popular election of the chief executive of each member state. And since, in this model, the decisions made at the international level are presumably confined to the behavior of nation-states, the interests of people and of different segments of the people in all states are collapsed into the single interest of the member nation-states.[3] The only quasi-citizens in the decision making of one state are the chief executives of the other states in the organization.

Such a simplification was never a good description of the true situation, but certainly in the current environment it does not describe the reality of making decisions in one country about issues that affect the collective status of the supranational organization or substantial interests in other members of the union. The realities of transnational political integration fall very short of creating even a central government similar to the federal system of the United States. Yet policies emerge, and people are affected. And where policies take shape, the reality is that politics is carried out, information is produced, problems are analyzed, people are consulted, and pressures are brought to bear transnationally.[4] What constitutes democratic performance in these emerging systems, and what institutions do or could do to promote these democratic decision in the interests of the people affected, is still in dispute.[5]

The most dramatic examples of transnational polities are the governments in formation—the United Nations, the European Union, and regional economic authorities like the North American Free Trade Agreement (NAFTA) and the Common Market of the South (Mercado Común del Sur; MERCOSUR)—all partial and specialized in different ways. There are also political action systems in formation, which include the sorts of representative links we have been discussing. Examples are major economic organizations, human rights advocacy groups, transnational jurists, and even entertainers who consider themselves part of a transnational political system. If a decision is pending on the establishment of international financial norms, much action bypasses the political systems of individual countries, but involves banks, economists, and major trading companies. Do they constitute "citizens" of the international organization? That category is only slowly developing legally even in the EU, while the political actions of groups and the decision-making power of the central authority is growing. In our terms, the core citizenry of Europe has yet to be established, except indirectly as the citizens of each of the member states. From the standpoint of the central decision makers, the networks of links to the people they have to respond to and get approval and compliance from have gone beyond the leaders of the member states to a complex set of people of the member states linked through some incipient political parties and many organizations active at the trans-European level.

It is possible to think of the evolution of the EU as the halting steps toward building a European nation-state. If that is the case, then the incipient links will become more and more institutionalized as they come to resemble those in the modern democratic nation-state. But perhaps there is a new norm built around the current fluid situation: the lines of representation are being formed beyond the borders of any single nation-state. In other words, not only are there many internationalizing, even "globalizing," modern states that must find ways to represent quasi-citizens, but the very core of the decision-making structure may not fit the comprehensive state model we have known since the eighteenth century. Decision centers may be more ad hoc, more changeable. And democratic performance may be even more complicated.

This situation raises a new issue: Will the nation-state remain the dominant form of political organization that it has been for several centuries? I ask this question here because it seems of a piece with broadening our consideration of citizenship to include both core and quasi-citizens.

In the midst of this rapidly changing situation, the democratic institutions of any single state must develop links between quasi-citizens and decision makers that go far beyond its own core citizenry. A highly dynamic set of quasi-citizens have to be heard and listened to and have the power to do significant damage. They include other governments, international agencies, citizens of other countries, and the organizations that seek to secure "decisions" by the sometimes amorphous decision makers of the whole community.

A current example is the European debt crisis, in which the choices made by, say, Greece will be "good" for Greeks only to the extent that Greece can predict the likely reactions of Germany and Britain (among other countries) and of the European and international financial institutions. Doing that requires that the decision makers reach out, much as they do to their own core citizenry, assessing preferences and the likelihood of punitive or supportive reaction. The priorities of the decision makers may be for the Greeks, but the instruments of representation must extend beyond Greece.

The rules and norms, perhaps laws, that guide and regulate the decision makers of the primary polity in reaching out to this complex of quasi-citizens are the existing institutions that shape the system's sensitivity to the factors in the transnational community that will have an impact on the effectiveness and justice of the policy decisions made.

Beyond their role in international organizations, quasi-citizens and governments in other jurisdictions play an important part in the structure of decision making by a country that has occupied or colonized another country. The history of colonization is replete with examples. The rationale of conquering nations in the past few centuries has been that they are bringing benefits to the colonized country: prosperity, democracy, civilization, the true religion, and/or an opening to the rest of the world. Often, of course, a more powerful reason is to exploit the resources or dominate the country for the glory it brings. Whatever the motivations and consequences, the politics of making decisions in the colonizing/invading country involves the expansion of representative links. To rule in the interests of the core citizens back "home," the colonial or military government must become sensitive to the preferences and situations of the people in the occupied country. To make any headway, in either improving or exploiting, the dominant government must know what the people of the country are thinking, how they will react, and under what conditions they will comply with rules—all of which are similar to what the decision makers have to know about their own core constituency. If a colonial or an occupying government wants to establish a democracy, it faces the same challenges as the reformers of democracy that are the subject of this book.

The people of an occupied or a colonized country are quasi-citizens of the colonizing nation—without the priority status, long-term identification, or comprehensive involvement of the core citizenry. The myth that the colonizers know everything they must know without building ongoing communication is as false as is the idea that populist dictators know their people well enough not to have to speak with them.

Similarly, the notion that occupation or colonization is a question of foreign policy and that the core citizens of the colonizing country will leave decision making to the executive is potentially dangerous to their welfare. In fact, it is less and less accurate. Business and financial interests develop their own networks, intercultural organizations grow, and a variety of domestic groups—from charitable agencies to religious missionaries—

become involved. And all these "private" entities will have their own input into the official policy of the occupying nation. Although concern for the welfare of the population of the occupied country will be a part of the rhetoric and of major concern to many observers, the blurred lines of influence will have serious ramifications for the representative system of the occupying country as well. Representative democratic institutions in the dominating country require that the links into the population of the colonized country are sophisticated, adaptable, and accurate in order to serve the core citizenry of the "home" country.

The military occupations by the United States of Japan and Germany after World War II, of Korea and Vietnam in the 1950s and 1960s, and now of Iraq and Afghanistan illustrate the complexities. But they also show the necessity of seeing the representative democratic system—in this case, of the United States—as including connections with the people of those countries. Whatever the wisdom of the initial invasions—obviously, much contested in the cases of Vietnam, Iraq, and Afghanistan—the benefits to the core citizenry of the United States depend on knowledge of and the compliance of the local population. Even though these occupations were intended to be temporary and not to completely supplant the local political system, links are important. Some come through "intelligence"; some, through opinions of experts; some, through contacts with local people selected to be leaders; some through contacts with local organizations by diplomats and military personnel; some through contacts with local groups or individuals by that nongovernmental and international organizations. It is a mix that has many of the elements that legislators and other decision makers in the United States use to connect to their own core constituencies.[6]

In this part of the book, I have emphasized the need to think about the institutionalization of quasi-citizens and their governments in the representative democratic decision-making process. The objective is not to implement the traditional conceptions of democratic representation, in any of its standard models, but to show where they are lacking. If we look at what is factually tied into the process of making decisions and necessary to make laws and policies in the interest of the people, we must expand our view of democratic institutions.

One way to think about this discussion is that the concepts of participation and democracy must be distinguished from each other. Many core citizens participate rarely in decision making, while many quasi-citizens do so frequently. Simply increasing core citizens' involvement will not deal with corruption, reckless presidents and prime ministers, social and economic inequality, and indecision in the face of crisis. The reforms that should be considered must include those that shape the real processes that include quasi-citizens who do not have the standing to participate in the classic institutions. Rather than try to include them in those models, I believe, we need new thinking about the identity of the institutions that promote representative democracy. Elections, parliaments of elected deputies, lobbying interest groups, and political parties are unquestionably essential for democracy, but, I argue, not enough.

Next we turn to another aspect of democratic representation—the links that connect this complex set of "people" to the decision-making process—and uncover other challenges for reformers.

PART III

THE LINKS

5

CONNECTING PEOPLE AND
DECISION MAKERS

D oes social networking bypass and undercut the institutional links between the people and the decision makers? Does the lack of organization in a group such as Occupy Wall Street mean that, short of staging some sort of revolution, it is inevitably blocked from influencing decisions? Do the personal friendships that Bill Clinton or David Cameron rely on for financial support and private information subvert democracy?

Another set of concerns for those seeking democratic reform are that existing channels of communication have characteristics—the changeability of organization and the salience of personal ties—that are unacknowledged in the traditional models of representation and that apparently undermine them. Reform has to confront and shape them, not ignore or prevent them.

Links concern the communication of information, material support, threats and rewards, promises and demands between the people and the decision makers. They are at the core of any representative democratic system, any system that claims to produce policies and laws in the interests of the people. As laid out in chapter 1, they include two-way communication of information and the rewards and punishments that hold decision makers accountable to the people.

Minimalist criteria for democracy downplay the significance of multiple means of interaction.[1] The people communicate politically through elections, they say, which either accept or reject leaders. Many conceptions of "representation," too, downplay the significance of active communication. According to them, the meaning of "representation" emphasizes the separation that makes representation necessary, but not ongoing. Some suggest that similarities between the represented and the representative obviate the necessity of their talking with each other much.[2] Women represent women; Kurds represent Kurds. Others focus on the distance between a representative and the people who are being represented, which makes communication between them difficult and even counterproductive. A diplomat is sent to a faraway land to handle the interests of her country. A legislative representative is elected and goes to the capital city to engage in governing, while the voter remains at home and involved with his own life without the bother of communicating with his deputy in any but the most episodic fashion.[3] Or the emphasis may be on the difference in knowledge and skills between the represented and the representative, which limits the significance of interaction. A lawyer is an agent who handles matters that the client does not have the competence to do. The leaders of a political party act for the people on the basis of their greater knowledge of the historical forces shaping their followers' conditions. Communication in such cases is limited to broad strategic questions or declarations from above. Some "populist" leaders claim to identify so strongly with their people that they are able to represent them without consulting them in any way, except during public festivals of acclamation.

Obvious facts about actual decision makers make these conceptualizations of representation marginally useful in describing the relationship between decision makers and the people. At best, they may refer to workarounds when communication is difficult; at worst, rationalizations for dictatorship. There are far too many interests at stake for members of the decision-making elites to reflect them all. To inform and punish decision makers who do not perform in the public interest, elections are far too blunt an instrument to achieve any sensitivity to the people's interests in the flow of decisions to be made. And although politicians have skills that make them different from ordinary people, even lawyers require active, continual communication with their clients to be good legal representatives.

It is inconceivable that any set of decision makers, however well intentioned and capable, could rule in the people's interest for any significant period of time without receiving ongoing information about the people's needs and preferences. It is impossible, too, that the people could know what to want—what problems face the nation and what opportunities are available to solve them—without information from the decision makers. "Representation" takes place in this interchange of information. And experience shows that a system of rewards and punishments, through which the people hold the decision makers accountable, is necessary for any democracy to endure.

The links between the people and the decision makers include the transfer of goods and money, as well as physical interactions ranging from handshakes and cheers to attacks and assassinations. But the overwhelmingly most important element of the links is information. Political action has long been defined in terms of talking, language, and communicating information. The links include face-to-face exchanges; public meetings; newspapers, radio, and television, and the constantly evolving Internet. The conventional name given to the press and broadcast outlets—the "media"—emphasizes this connecting function.

The institutions that make a decision-making process democratic are those that shape this talk in ways that promote effective and just outcomes. There are many opportunities for miscommunication, deception, misunderstanding, and manipulated information—in both directions.

The conventional models of representative institutions described in chapter 1 are centered on these links. The deputy model concentrates on elections as the guarantor of accountability and the communication between the deputy and the constituents as the main channel to be described (and regulated). The partisan model introduces the idea of an organization to mediate the links. In a system with strong political parties, the parties organize the debate, the media, the legislature, and the elections. The accountability mechanisms range from electoral to cooperation or opposition during the legislative process. Parties teach their members as well as learn from them. In the pluralistic models, the organizations of the interest groups inform the decision makers and learn from or teach their members, relying on mobilization for elections or demonstrations. Their role in accountability lies in exposure, fund-raising, and public confrontation.

The next two facts about politics that demand a new agenda in thinking about democratic institutions take the form of questioning two assumptions that underlie all of the conventional models: that a desirable system establishes a stable set of links built around organizations and that beyond personal contacts between deputies and constituents, personal connections undermine democracy.

6

ORGANIZATIONS
AND THEIR ALLIANCES
CHANGE RAPIDLY

*The way networks of organizations form, decay, and reconfigure themselves for each
issue is important for the effectiveness and justice of decisions.*

Fact 3

Organizations and networks of organizations do a great deal to shape the communication between the people and the decision makers. Some communication between them is done directly: constituents visit their legislators' offices or send e-mail messages; voters meet their representatives or other candidates during electioneering; and constituents and their legislators get together at public or private fund-raising events. Much communication is done through the mass media. A major element in managing the personal and the media interactions is the many political organizations that shape, mobilize, and focus the messages between the people and the decision makers. Political organizations are sets of people who come together around some identity, ranging from self-interest to adherence to a principle, or merely a mechanism to perform a function, such as put up candidates for office. They build a means to communicate with one another to coordinate their actions. They build channels to broader audiences in order to mobilize support, generate ideas, energize allies, and build links to decision makers to pressure, influence, and gain information on opportunities.

Political organizations are crucial intermediaries in any representative system.

In the form of parties and interest groups, political organizations have been at the center of the basic models of representation. Some theorists have rejected the idea of any political organization at all on the ground that it fosters division among governments or people,[1] and there is an underlying negative connotation of divisive "factions" in many people's use of the terms "political parties" and "special interest groups."[2] But political organizations are so common and central to the political process that reforms of the institutions of representative democracy often focus almost exclusively on their practices. Taking some examples from American politics, there have been calls for "more responsible political parties," restrictions on former legislators serving as lobbyists for interest groups, reforms to promote primaries within parties, rules to limit campaign donations by private groups to parties or candidates' support committees, requirements for "equal time" in the media for parties, and so forth.

The group and organizational aspect of the links crucial to representation is so complex and dynamic that before we directly address the problems of reform, I shall discuss the types of organizations and the patterns they form. Among organizations relevant to politics, political parties do stand out, mobilizing people and mobilizes pressures for decisions: helping to form cabinets, organizing the legislature, and the like. The party system organizes the conflicts: establishing the government and the opposition, running the elections, aligning newspapers, and so on. Political parties have played a key role in shaping the communication between the people and the decision makers, especially in periods of great polarization. At the other end of the spectrum of involvement in politics, social and do-it-yourself groups such as sports clubs and private museum organizations become political occasionally when they are involved in promoting laws about property or government subsidies. In between these poles are groups dedicated to the political process in varying degrees, such as those devoted mainly to analyzing and proposing reforms in health services aimed directly to hospitals and, as part of their effort, promoting reform of the government's policies on health care.

Finding a name that refers to all of these groups in general is complicated. Although the label "nongovernmental organization" is used to describe many of them, integration into the government varies independently of integration into the policy-making process.[3] A government agency for meteorological research may be nonpolitical, while an independent center for economic research may be highly political, since it is interested exclusively in influencing law and policy. The general designation of "civil society" is used to denote the sphere in question, and since I wish to emphasize their organizational qualities, I will call them "civil society associations."

The variety of perspectives on the importance of these associations can be illustrated by a brief discussion of four classic visions of their character and role. These can be designated as the Madisonian, Tocquevillian, Marxist, and the Bentley-Truman pluralist visions.

· James Madison, in *The Federalist Papers*, called attention to the multiplicity of "factions," by which he seemed to mean the groupings of decision makers who promoted their own interests and worked against others who had different interests.[4] He defended the new Constitution as a way to avoid any one of the factions from taking over the government. He did not try to outlaw them, as Jean-Jacques Rousseau might have advocated. Rather, assuming that the interests of these factions were inherently local, he argued that a large state, such as would be established with the new Constitution, would lead to their proliferation and lessen the possibility of any one dominating.

In the post–World War II period, when scholars identified the prewar partisan polarization of European politics as a major cause of the tragedy of the rise of the Nazis and the war, the Madisonian vision was extended and transformed to point to factors that could have prevented that polarization: the multiplicity of interest groups that, by virtue of memberships cutting across those of other organizations, could have provided a natural barrier to everyone choosing up sides.

· The Tocquevillian vision, in contrast, imagines civil society associations as clubs of people whose members come together to work, worship, play, or politic.[5] Alexis de Tocqueville and many who have followed him were interested how these groups socialize citizens into cooperative, trusting behavior that has the side effect of making democratic institutions work. This view became popular in the late twentieth century, as a strategy to build or rebuild democracies. A vibrant civil society would create the necessary trust and practice in democratic skills and would provide the basis for competitive party systems and peaceful elections. In this view, it is not so important that these associations be organized around common demands (which would make them interest groups). Rather, they may be established to pursue a wide variety of often nonpolitical activities—from parent-teacher associations to football and bowling clubs. The expansion of the number of such association builds what many call "social capital."[6]

• The Marxist perspective emphasizes Karl Marx's vision of mobilizing people around not just common interests, but a theory of change and a program for bringing it about.[7] The most dramatic incarnations of this vision are revolutionary movements and their political parties on the left and right. Having a mission and a theory became the definition of a "real" movement in the polarized atmosphere of the first half of the twentieth century. Many embraced the rhetoric of a broad solidaristic movement meant to triumph over a historically determined oppression. Although belief in the sort of total historical transformation that Marx had in mind is less encountered now, the idea of contentious groups hoping to achieve specific goals and decisive change by means of political action is very common. It is at the heart of the social-movement model of representation. Each woman's group, neighborhood organization, labor union, biodiversity preservation committee, and anti-tax and libertarian movement can be regarded not as representing an interest to be folded into the deliberative decision-making process, but as working for a "change in the system." The collapse of authoritarian regimes in eastern Europe, Latin America, and now the Middle East is seen as the result of actions taken by transformational movements: pro-democracy groups, alliances of victims of repression, and human rights organizations. Many feel that demonstrations by movements that represent the oppressed are the only way to address inequality. The "anti-institutional" bias of this approach has often made it difficult to recognize that many organizations that use anti-Establishment rhetoric are a component of the representative system. The development of institutions to represent the people organized in this way is a challenge because of the need for a way to channel the energies involved and avoid the stalemates and breakdowns that are possible from clashing transformational positions.

• The Bentley-Truman perspective, associated with the work of Arthur Bentley and David Truman,[8] is at the base of the interest-group model described in chapter 1: people come together around a single interest in order to lobby for decisions favorable to that interest. It is a perspective more congenial than the Marxist to the idea of integrating organizations into an ongoing system of decision making. There is a similarity between this model and the way markets are thought to behave. The belief is that a system can work productively and stably if people are allowed to formulate their own interests and act to realize them. This view does not have the "contentiousness" of the Marxist vision, the sociocultural function of the Tocquevillian model, or the divisiveness implied in the Madisonian perspective.

The association of the pluralist model with democracy has diverse sources. A common definition of modern "totalitarian "governments is regimes that seek "total control" over groups in civil society. Pluralism is considered to be a sign of democracy, as well as a guarantee against the sort of single-faction dominance that can lead to the overthrow of democratic regimes. The United States has long been considered to have exceptionally large number of interest groups and had a claim to attention as the most powerful state left standing after World War II and the Cold War, and therefore a leading democracy. Further, a common identification of the open competition of democratic politics with the open competition of the market led many to find virtue in the development of autonomous enterprises, and that virtue was transferred subtly to autonomous political groups.

In each of these perspectives, civil society associations are a major part of the representative regime because they shape the links between the people and the decision makers. Pluralist groups mobilize people around a particular interest that is communicated to the decision makers. In the "social capital" version of the Tocquevillian model, the experience of being members of an organization brings citizens out of their self-centered "individualism" and equips them for participation in the political process. The Marxist or social-movement type of organization teaches people what they want and mobilizes them to bring it about. All work with common interests and create new bases for articulating preferences and bringing pressure. Many citizens count on them for (or are led to believe) the information, the perspectives, and the understanding of opportunity costs necessary for informed participation; the decision makers rely on them in order to make informed decisions. The preferences of the citizens are shaped and are articulated to decision makers by these groups.

On the accountability side, associations can punish and reward decision makers in many ways. They can provide or withhold resources for elections; they can help make or break reputations; they can contribute to creating or disrupting the "connections" that politicians rely on. If they do their job well (from the point of view of the system and those they are representing), the failure of the leaders to perform can be exposed. Civil society associations can play a major role in holding the representatives accountable.

The most obvious fact about politics with respect to these groups lies in their multiplicity and diversity. Many have suggested that they represent the key to a new form of democratic government, based presumably on voluntary participation and grassroots organization. Some have argued that democracy would be promoted by inserting some version of these associations into governance in particular arenas, such as health care, environmental protection, and local budgeting.[9]

Of course, for all the association of nongovernmental groups with democracy, they can also have negative effects. Creating and running these associations takes resources, and richer social strata may fund powerful and influential groups that come to accentuate inequality. Reckless policies may be more common if governments or special interests have the capacity to foster sympathetic policy research that can be isolated from view. The influence of lobbyists may encourage corruption. The cacophony of contentious movements and demonstrations—if they do not lead to the desired outcomes of change—may block policies that might otherwise deal with pressing problems.

From another perspective, many interest groups appear to have very narrow or inflexible constituencies—for example, a group lobbying for coal-mining companies or a "not-in-my-backyard" (NIMBY) set of neighbors opposing the location of a rehabilitation center for addicts. They represent only a small set of interests of each of the members, and the model of "citizenship" in the organization is faulty. If a proposal were to emerge that changed the issue from one rehabilitation center to the reconstruction of a section of the city, other concerns about education, parks, and policing would change the interests of some members of the NIMBY organization and thus the set of relevant people.

Some have suggested that promoting internal democracy in civil society associations is crucial, likening each nongovernmental organization to a polity with decision makers and citizens. But making lobbying organizations, environmental policy think tanks, parent-teacher associations, soccer clubs, volunteer fire departments, Web-based watchdogs on politicians' scandals, and energy-company lobbying groups more responsive to a specific set of members may be counterproductive. The interests of these groups are almost certainly broader or narrower than the suggested image of their "citizens" suggests. To what constituency does a climate-change action group respond? To which set of members should a set of decision makers and activists in an organization promoting rights for racial minorities or illegal migrants be made answerable? They are seeking to make the wider political process more responsive to a range of people in these categories, almost certainly much wider than that of the members of the specific organization.

What would make civil society associations have more democratic results?[10] Another common approach is to have confidence in the unregulated actions of the people to create necessary new organizations. Freedom of association is held to be the key, combined with transparency. In the case of the totalitarian regimes of the early twentieth century, this viewpoint is convincing, although it is a good deal less convincing as a remedy for dealing with the weakness of the current democracies, in which the proliferation of associations seems endemic.

So what other approaches to reforming institutions might work? The most obvious is the direct regulation of the associations. Establishing special tax categories for them, drawing up rules against "buying votes" by lobbyists, passing laws against employing violence as a means to convey their messages, guaranteeing free speech for them, and devising formal or informal norms for equal time in the media are among the proposals that deserve discussion. There is clearly much to do in the way of these "conventional" reforms.

But regulating the groups is a challenge because of their fluidity. The effort to limit contributions to political campaigns and the role of lobbyists runs into the creativity of the people who run these associations in finding loopholes and wrangling special considerations in order to pursue their goals, which are legal even if their methods are not. Sometimes it seems hopeless.

THE LOW COST OF RECONFIGURING ALLIANCES OF CIVIL SOCIETY ASSOCIATIONS

Devising rules for civil society associations to follow that would produce democratic outcomes is complicated not only by the deviousness of the leaders of many of these organizations, but also by the fact that the ensemble of such groups does not have the enduring quality of, for example, a party system.

I do not think that we can make any headway without taking into account a major fact about them that has not been the focus until now. Contrary to the implied assumption of the various perspectives, although some associations endure for many years, many come and go. Even more important, their alliances are even more transient. Because any individual group is likely to have limited power, alliances are made among civil society associations and with political parties, government agencies, and prominent personalities. They are formed to deal with more or less specific goals, and when they are achieved (or changed, postponed, or abandoned), the alliances disappear, often to be replaced by others to deal with new issues or opportunities. And this dynamism is accelerating because civil society associations and their alliances are increasingly inexpensive to form and increasingly disposable.

The political shape of civil society associations and their alliances with political parties, government agencies, civil institutions, and prominent personalities—so crucial to their ability to mobilize segments of the population in order to shape laws or policy—can make a system democratic or not. Such a dynamic system is capable of becoming—although not inevitably fated to become—a highly adaptive system, identifying specific problems, drawing stakeholders into meaningful dialogue, linking to public and private research centers to review findings and propose workable solutions, educating the public, and applying sanctions to politicians who fail to respond to just demands. They could be the perfect set of links in a representative system.

The frequent reconfiguration of decision-making networks, however, may be chaotic or manipulated in such a way as to obfuscate, mislead, and weaken the mobilization of energies to deal with even those problems that have been correctly recognized. Chaotic processes will fail to formulate any effective decisions, much less just ones. A common theme among those who are skeptical of the contribution of civil society associations to democracy is that the people with the greatest ability to form them—presumably the rich and already powerful—will have the opportunity to influence policy in their favor, accentuating the bias and inequality in the results. The rapid construction and reconstruction of organizations and networks means that their advantages and access are multiplied.

Counteracting that danger, at least in part, is another development. The advantages enjoyed by the rich and powerful shrink when forming associations or alliances among them becomes inexpensive in time, money, and energy. While many of the issues discussed in this book have been present for a long time, the dynamic quality of the civil society associations has taken on a new dimension. Specialized groups came and went before, but the new technologies of communication make the change of civil society organizations a frequent occurrence. New links, new organizations, new fund-raising efforts, and new calls for action can be formulated in a very short period of time and abandoned equally quickly. Communication is the soul of representation, so when something as profound as what is called the "digital revolution" occurs,[11] it is bound to have a powerful impact on the operations of politics. Bruce Bimber has plausibly argued that in the United States, several revolutions in communication technology—mail, the telegraph, the telephone, and mass media—brought about structural changes in American politics.[12] The digital revolution will surely do so as well.

The digital revolution is such a dynamic process that predicting even a short-run outcome would be foolish in the extreme. Many predictions of structural changes have been made, such as a dramatic expansion in participation, the fragmentation of the populace, and the instability of the system from overmobilization or a constant state of revolutionary change.[13] Most are extrapolations of short-term changes that do not survive the next transformation. But although it is difficult or even impossible to say where it is going, it is possible to see some consequences that present new challenges to the institutions that affect the representativeness of decision making.

DISPOSABLE ORGANIZATIONS AND NETWORKS

Those who hope to reform the institutions of representative democracy have to come to terms with the fact that organizations and the alliances among them are becoming disposable. We often assume that in this age of "mass politics," building a political organization requires great effort, much money, abundant energy, strict coordination, grunt work, and strategic planning. We believe that an organization needs resources, lines of command, a sort of bureaucracy, and a stable, participatory membership. And since well-established groups have the greatest "fixed investments," it is natural to assume that they are more able to prevail than are casually organized, informally structured, temporary groups. Like government bureaucracies and major corporations, they gain power as they grow, and the decision to abandon them is a major concession of defeat and involves the difficult process of unloading the investments, laying off the staff, and the like. The long histories of political parties, major corporate interest groups, and trade unions seem to underline the importance of these "fixed investments." But the investments change with the times, too, and become a drag on the system.

Mass electronic media and digital communications—radio, television, the Internet, and personal-networking sites—have changed the tools of organization and thus the conventional scenario recounted in the last paragraph. The global reach of the new technology, and yet the capacity to focus on very specific issues that affect a small, perhaps never before mobilized group, creates a new situation for politics. If a political organization is a mechanism to bring people together, provide a means of communication with one another, and coordinate their actions, then creating a political organization through digital technology is relatively inexpensive, changes the role of physical location as part of the identity of the organization, and transforms the definition of "participation." These qualities affect industry, government, the military, and all sorts of organizations beyond political associations. But they influence political organizations more than most others, since politics is close to being exclusively about coordination and communication. Social media—such as Facebook and Twitter—are even more "just" about talk, and their rise and spread only emphasizes the fluidity of the medium.

Digital communication has many effects on the shape and behavior of political organizations in the representative process (and thus the requirements for reform). It eases mobilization across borders. It facilitates the vast increase in access to knowledge about policies and their impacts (as discussed in chapter 9). And it makes possible the rapid reformulation and reconfiguration of civil society associations and their alliances. Digital communication changes what is required to reach out to and make alliances with other organizations, government agencies, or political parties. And it lowers the costs of abandoning any particular configuration. Digital communications makes civil society associations and their alliances much more "disposable."

By "disposable," I mean to emphasize the lack of intrinsic value of any particular formation beyond the particular task it was created to accomplish. Disposable products—from razors and napkins to biodegradable garbage bags and many children's toys—are extremely important when one is shaving and putting out the trash and challenging children, but they are inexpensive to make and not worth cleaning and reusing. The word "disposable" has a negative connotation for environmentalists because of the waste they presumably create, but that problem can be solved by making items recyclable as well as reusable.

What do advocacy Web sites and paper napkins have in common? Both are both easy to make (with the right technology), and after they serve their purpose, the elements (people, Internet connections, skills for the Web site, fibers for the paper) can be disassembled and made available for something else, almost surely not in the same configuration, but a different mix of elements, perhaps even for a very different purpose (a social-networking site or a cardboard box).

The digital revolution has reduced drastically the costs of the first steps in organizing politically—that is, how much money, knowledge, effort, and time it takes to begin a collective effort to influence the system. From the standpoint of the system, it has by no means reduced the total amount of time and resources spent on political communication. (If the media storms in recent elections and policy conflicts are an indication, the amounts of all resources have been multiplied.) The creation and re-creation of organizations go on constantly. And the process still takes skills, dedication, and effort.

But from the standpoint of a group that wants to advocate a law or policy, the methods are shifting—from establishing an office in a centrally located building, hiring secretaries, and setting up files and mailing operations, to constructing a Web site and developing a network of links with discussion sites, with interviews by its leaders with the press or on blogs,[14] and with social networks. It is a set of steps that can take place much more rapidly than before.

A group of people interested in securing legislation that would promote or require ecologically smart production and recycling programs in the packaging industry might arrange for an initial declaration in the media—television and the Internet—send e-mails to various mailing lists of potential supporters and donors, and get people in various cities to organize boycotts. They would link with various environmental and progressive groups, including labor unions, for publicity and support. They would contact sympathetic legislators to ask them to propose laws to regulate packaging. But if technical innovations changed the recyclability of some kinds of packaging, the policy of this group might shift to promote the production and purchase of some products rather than others. This might well lead to a change in the alliances. Labor unions might not be as enthusiastic in discriminating among companies based on their products, a new set of legislators who are connected with the environmental movement might be recruited, and different strategies for boycotts and consumer education would have to be developed, which might well require linking with different local groups.

Web sites, e-mail lists, and discussion boards are more flexibly selective than other methods of mobilization. This means that similarity is more important than proximity. It is far easier to find people with specific qualities, even if they are widely dispersed. A group might reach out very broadly for workers or conservatives, but it could also bring together homeowners with similar experiences with banks in Cleveland, the owners of pit bulls (or their neighbors), or the relatives of those killed on September 11. The selectivity of the Internet stems from its technology, which is refined and enhanced constantly by commercial users who want to identify and reach likely customers, or political figures who want to locate and reach likely supporters. This selectivity becomes stronger and stronger as various forms of databases become available.

Once it seemed that electronic communication would never supersede face-to-face communication because it could not supply the give-and-take of an organization and political meetings. But the "nodes" of like-minded actors on the Internet, however, have become more and more interactive. E-mail, blogs, and wiki-style Web sites; comment techniques; and virtual worlds like Second Life—all of which seem to emerge (and disappear) more and more frequently—make possible the kind of discussion and debate that are intrinsic to political organizing.

Technology is evolving too quickly to assess the significant differences between electronic interaction and face-to-face communication. Perhaps the differences may be greater anonymity? an emphasis on instant reactions, rather than reflection over days or longer? a loss of affect? the infection of an "advertising mode" where "lies of omission" are accepted? Perhaps the differences will surface when the current phase, which emphasizes typing over speaking, develops into a multi-media style, with audio and video interactions. But all existing and likely changes will increase the interactive and targeted quality of the links and the speed with which the subject of discussion, agitation, pressure, and action can be changed.

The "disposability" of political groups that electronic mobilization makes possible presents a whole series of new challenges for reforming representative institutions. It makes it necessary to rethink Madisonian factiousness, Tocquevillian social capital, Marxist solidarity, and Bentley-Truman pluralism. Reformers will have to find ways to counteract the Madisonian divisiveness that is so easily created through electronic communication. They will have to find ways to make social media create the sort of trust and public commitment that Tocqueville saw in civil society associations. They will have to find ways to promote the conversion of the energy of Marxist-style social movements into responsive and adaptive movements. They will have to find ways to make the rapid-reorientation organizations still produce the breadth of interests in society in a just fashion. Because Bentley-Truman pluralism was never good at suggesting how poor and underclass populations can be represented in the political system, the question will be whether the new flexibility offered by digital technology produces more equal access or less, and what might be done about it.

What makes it likely that the "nodes" of political action will emerge at the right time to address significant problems and counteract tendencies toward systematic inequality? Unequal access to the Web is a basic problem, but given the rate of expansion of such access, the problems will become more subtle.

Needless to say, every one of these aspects of the new forms of communication can work against good representation as well as for it. Rapidly changing nodes of influence may fracture any serious effort to tackle broad, long-term questions. The emphasis on information can become elitist and obfuscating. Self-organizing efforts to deal with problems may respond to market-like signals that fail to respond to long-term needs, much as markets often create inequality.

This is an arena that requires rules and regulations, informal standards and customary practices to shape the outcomes. The old agenda of reform is still relevant, but needs expansion. Reforms should deal not only with how the individual organizations can be structured more democratically or behave more transparently. Nor should reforms concern only the relationship between individual organizations and the government, as in preventing buying influence and special access to secrets. These are important and significant reforms. But my point here is that reformers will need a new agenda, since creating new organizations and networks of new and old ones is a much more constant process than the old models suggested. How they are constructed initially matters a great deal because their impact is of the moment: whether they include directly or indirectly all the stakeholders (foreign and domestic), whether they tap into the most relevant information to deal with an issue, and whether they establish an appropriate decision-making process. These are the areas where the institutions of representative democracy have to be shaped and reformed.

7

PERSONAL NETWORKS
ARE IMPORTANT

Personal ties persist and have positive as well as negative consequences for the efficiency and justice of decisions.

Fact 4

Personal networks are important elements of politics. Their persistence and functionality constitute another fact about politics that needs formal or informal regulation to enhance representative democracy. While many of the dimensions discussed in chapter 6 are changing rapidly, personal networks have been characteristic of politics from the beginning. Friendships, family connections, school ties, back-scratching, romantic alliances, personal loyalties, oaths to help one another whatever the circumstances, personal debts to be paid off in the future—these and many other connections between individuals have always been close to the core of politics. It is possible to describe all social patterns, even highly formal organizations, in terms of "network theory," mapping the various sorts of links among people. I am taking a narrower, more conventional definition of personal ties, in which there is an element of solidarity with another person with mutual expectations of asymmetric exchange based on a relationship extrinsic to the political activity in question. A promise of votes for favors or services not as direct payment but for the sake of family ties or graduate-school connections are within this definition. Relationships between people that stem from membership in an organization or shared material interests are not. Rather, they manifest a bond based on exchange, shared experiences, or emotion, including love.

In nonpolitical situations, personal ties are prized—love, loyalty, friendship, family, and community. But liberal political thought has long considered personal ties as anathema, or at least unlikely to be a positive influence in promoting the will of the people. They hint at favoritism and privilege, against which the liberal and social revolutions of the past three centuries have struggled. Real and manufactured family ties were the glue of the aristocratic elites of the ancien régime. Even worse, for many the hallmark of the pre-liberal societies was the feudal relation built into the personal tie between king and vassals and, at the base, between lord and serf. Once, only traditional, "particularistic" links based on personal obligations were prized. Family and personal ties were lauded by many, from Confucius to Cicero to Montaigne. But in modern times, personal obligations are likened either to domination—the relationships between master and slave, political boss and followers, and Mafia don and soldiers—or to ways to avoid the universalist obligations of the law.

Negative terms are used to describe these networks: "clientelism," "cronyism," "nepotism," and "political favoritism." Some labels, such as "Mafia" and "gang," reflect the common association of personal networks with criminal activity or, at the least, corruption and subversion of the law.[1] Democracy, particularly in its liberal form, seems synonymous with the rule of law, universal rights and obligations, and merit-based hiring. Whether they take the form of patterns of personal dependence or webs of "fraternal" ties, personal networks seem alien to the modern, liberal spirit and thus antipathetic to democratic representation.[2]

Yet personal networks are everywhere. They penetrate, support, complement, substitute for, anticipate, and sometimes corrupt civil society associations, bureaucracies, political parties, corporations, and all sorts of legal arrangements. Many forms of personal networks are important to democratic systems and to representation within them. "Policy networks" constituted by groups and organizations often result from and are kept together with personal connections.[3] These networks are important to the deliberation process on many topics, especially new ones, and may be indispensable for identifying problems and solutions.[4] When a new problem emerges, friends and old colleagues are often the first people contacted, and from these links may emerge a policy network of organizations that address the issue.[5]

The "teams" formed around leading politicians and based, at least in part, on personal loyalty may be more central to establishing and defending coherent policies than political parties, government bureaucracies, and interest groups. Nongovernmental organizations (NGOs) may begin as, and possibly remain, a group of friends from a professional school who have a common purpose and may become crucial to introducing ideas from a non-Establishment perspective.[6] Networks that respond to new challenges or opportunities—composed of people in government agencies, civil society associations, policy think tanks, and interested business groups—may be structured around existing organizations or common interests. But often they are grounded on such nonpolitical bases as shared experiences (attending the same university, serving together in the military), or an exchange of goods and services.

Personal connections are clearly changing with the growth of person-to-person communication on the Internet. Although modernity may have brought principles of universalism, the increasing capacity to link instantly and tentatively allows experimentation with new alliances. The use of terms like "families," "communities," "followings," and "friends" to describe electronic relationships that can be intimate or span the globe does not necessarily mean that personal networks are the wave of the future. But it clearly suggests that despite the association of personal networks with traditional ties, such as those among family members, they are a dynamic element in the contemporary scene. It seems to be assumed that ties made through social networks like Twitter, Facebook, LinkedIn, and texting are more fragile and less permanent than face-to-face connections, but the technology is constantly changing and there clearly has not been enough experience with them to be able to make such a judgment.

Including something as fluid and "behind the scenes" as personal networks may seem strange in a book devoted to examining how political institutions might be reformed. The significance of family or friendship ties is often covered in analyses of political culture, not political institutions. But the term "institutions" should include not only formal, legal prescriptions, but also informal ones. A legal prohibition on nepotism is a relevant formal rule, but the practices of universities in fostering networking among their graduates is also a commonly followed informal norm. The proscription of payments to a mistress or a kept boy by a political leader is usually not by law, but publicity may make it enforceable.

The pattern of personal links in organizations can lead to many kinds of pathology, which would be the job of reformed institutions to avoid, whether by law or by accepted norm, if possible. Sometimes personal links influence negatively the groups around influential political actors. Friendship with a leader may not be best criterion to use when selecting the people who govern a country, hence the emphasis on promotion based on merit. Formal rules designed to ensure advancement because of achievement are a feature of modern government. Some balance of the leader's choice and approval by others aims at limiting the leader's ability to select incompetents, while allowing him or her to build a "team."

When a network of people is forming to identify a problem, consider and generate solutions, and suggest laws or policies to implement them, it may fail because the behavior of the members of competing teams linked personally to different leaders or teams linked personally to one leader but competing for his approval may lead to stalemate. Proposals based on personal ties are difficult to compromise or manipulate because secret deals are made rather than joint deliberation undertaken. The personal network, often the followers of a single person, may be tied to and dependent on that person in ways that disrupt the give-and-take required for rationally dealing with issues. Many experiences of "partisanship" in contemporary policy making in the United States illustrate the dangers. Although disguised as a dispute over principle, in fact partisanship is part of the old game of pushing forward a personal network to dominate a debate. At a local level, the pathologies of personal networks might show through personal rivalries (perhaps exacerbated by competition for electoral success) that prevent residents of an urban neighborhood from uniting to form an organization to promote their representation in a city-sponsored development project.

Another pathology of personal networks is revealed in interpretations of the disaster of the wars initiated by the United States in Iraq and Afghanistan. The Bush administration's imposition of tight security and demands of loyalty from the White House "team" had much to do with preventing the policy makers' interaction with a range of opinion and expertise held in different segments of the public. More openness may have uncovered the errors of fact, theory, and interpretation that had much to do with the decision to go to war. Conspiracy theories proposed by observers who explain everything that goes wrong in terms of malevolent personal "cabals" behind events that they do not like can be caricatures of such a pathology, but it does not mean that the core insight is wrong.

The potential positive consequences of personal networks for representative politics are not so often discussed. The advantages of trust reinforced through family ties—for example, when a CEO appoints a cousin to a responsible position, as opposed to hiring only on the basis of demonstrated performance—was key in the mid-twentieth-century discussions about family firms and family links to banks in Latin America and elsewhere.[7] The beneficial functions of the political-boss system in American cities for the social integration of immigrants in the early twentieth century, despite the taint of corruption, is another example.[8]

More often, the benefits are evident to the participants, but invisible to others. The personal connections between the staff of various NGOs working on similar problems—say, childhood disease or AIDS prevention—are often the channel for the dissemination of knowledge and innovative approaches. Personal connections may also be the basis on which alliances are built to get legal support or funding.

Personal networks may be the vehicle through which society, so to speak, tests the waters for the development of more "regular" organizations or links. They may, as in the NGO example, provide the initial stages in the formation of a more stable interest group or even a political party, reflecting new or unrepresented groups in the system. They may provide channels to represent quasi-citizens. In the background of every major political party, revolutionary movement, or civil society association surely was a network of individuals, brought together by ties other than those that would become the raison d'être of the organizations they founded.[9] While this may be regarded as merely an interesting historical fact, the importance of such path breaking is dramatically increased in a world of rapid mobilization based in part on the cost reductions for action provided by the Internet and on the continual reconfiguration of civil society associations.

Although as mentioned earlier, the "teams" that coordinate and guide the top levels of decision making have a potential for negative consequences, such as installing incompetents in high office, they also have important positive impacts on the representative system. The best known are the "kitchen cabinets," "cliques," or "wise men" who advise presidents and prime ministers, but they can be found in corporations, government agencies, and any other large-scale organization. They may or may not overlap with the formally designated offices—the cabinet, the executive office, the boards of directors—established to counsel decision makers. The informal, personal links often take precedence because what is crucial is not the formal running of the institution, but the combination of trust, confidence, and competence.

The role of personal ties in coordinating efforts in firms and government and similar organizations are, I suspect, taken for granted. Why, though, do I regard it as crucial for representing the people in a democratic system? The personal links do not extend directly to "the people." Efforts by populist leaders to establish such a connection are rightly greeted with suspicion. But building on the notion developed in chapter 1 that representation is not accomplished by having a representative for each interest, the question becomes how the interests of the people in all their complexity can be acknowledged.

Linking diverse and changing interests to the decision-making process requires the constant reconstruction of the links. Personal networks can obviously be negative for equality when they support a narrow elite, such as leaders of large financial institutions fighting regulation. But the best possibility of sidestepping "entrenched interests" is through the flexibility of personal ties. Whistle-blowers who have connections with prosecutors or opposition leaders can call attention to corrupt practices. Government employees who have ties to college buddies in the press may break the silence about a reckless decision and force discussion in public. The personal friendships of people who taught at the same university may enable a coalition to begin forming to deal with a stalemate in a legislature.

What sorts of actions would prevent the negative consequences and enhance the positive contributions of personal networks? Passing anti-corruption legislation or anti-nepotism laws that threaten fines or establish oversight is one approach to deal with the negative side. But personal networks are built on informal relationships that can bypass the attempts at regulation by means of registries and reports.

On the positive side, what would encourage the construction of personal networks for exchanging information, exploring innovative approaches, trying out new policy-making themes, and experimenting with new services? What would encourage the development of personal networks for reaching out to newly defined groups, such as single mothers who lose their jobs or homeowners who lose their mortgages through new kinds of fraud? Formally established organizations might serve such groups better than informal personal networks, but what would encourage people to mobilize their friends to take the first step that might lead to the creation of those organizations? Computers and smartphones provide a base and make person-to-person connections and the formation of groups based on them much easier than it otherwise would be, although it is always possible that the ease of connection may foster the sort of casual links that do not lead to the development of formal organizations.

A great deal depends on informal rules. The norms that develop in group activities required in professional schools, the habits that are acquired in internships and early jobs, and the style of networking that exists in families, churches, schools, sports clubs, and local service organizations can either devolve into self-interested, exploitative attitudes or evolve into task-oriented, collective efforts that would serve the community in the end. Blind loyalty to friends or family may be bad, but no loyalty at all may be worse. The task of reformers must be to find ways to promote the best in personal connections.

A representative democracy is a political system in which the people engage in a two-way conversation with those who make decisions, in a way that produces laws and policies in the people's interest. In this part of the book, I have argued that the links through which that conversation takes place are much more varied, dynamic, and flexible than the classic accounts of the election of deputies, the actions of party systems, and the formation of pluralist groups would suggest. The process of construction and reconstruction of those links virtually changes the meaning of organization and calls attention to new technologies and enduring personal ties. Here is where the new agenda must take hold.

Next we turn to the targets of those links from the people: the policy- and lawmaking process, where decisions are made and the elements of the decision-making process come together. New challenges for democratic reformers emerge.

PART IV

THE DECISION MAKERS

8
===

LAW- AND POLICY MAKING

When contrasting positions are presented, supported by different facts and theories—for example, by an oil company and a fishermen's organization—about rules for the exploration for oil under the sea, what makes it possible to arrive at a decision that benefits both parties and the society? Does the fact that many issues are decided by administrative agencies after ad hoc conversations with "experts" and stakeholders, rather than by open debate in the legislature, mean that democracy is subverted? Does calling in academic experts mean that nongovernmental organizations and local on-the-ground people are under- or unrepresented?

The next facts about the political process that suggest lacunae in existing recipes for institutional reform have to do first with the weakness of explicit norms to make sure that when problems arise the information offered by competing sides is tested and productively debated so that decisions serve democratic ends. The second concerns the effort to shape law and policies when the work of decision making is done not in a single place (like a legislature) but in many working groups, personal networks, and special commissions.

But first we must consider some basic observations about the way law- and policy making is currently conceived. At the core of any political system, representative or not, are the processes that decide on the laws and polices to be adopted, implemented, and enforced. They turn the information about the preferences, demands, and needs of the people that is communicated to the decision makers into the laws and policies that either serve the people's interests or do not. They involve identifying problems; making proposals; assembling information about context; designating and linking stakeholders; conducting participant interaction (discussion, bargaining); arriving at conclusions; and promulgating, implementing, and reviewing the outcomes.

Classic models of decision making concentrate on the single point of "final," authoritative decision. The many steps are taken by a variety of people, but there is a strong pressure for thinking of them as being unified in a single process. Especially for legislation, the point of promulgation is crucial because establishing the law implies unity and an authoritative center. There must be a point at which a law becomes the law of the land, not merely a verbal principle. For decisions on policies that commit a polity's use of its resources, the need for a "final" point is not as clear-cut, since multiple agencies may interpret possibilities, adopt goals, and deploy resources— thus "making" policy. But there is pressure to coordinate, which implies a single final point for decisions where such coordination is managed.

In a polity dominated by a single political figure, the process of hearing demands, considering the realities, and choosing alternatives was thought to take place in the mind of that leader—an emperor, a monarch, a "philosopher king," or a chief executive. More realistically, it occurred within that person's inner circle—his confidants, staff, advisers, and ministers.

But with the development of liberal and representative governments, the process of decision making came to be identified with lawmaking. Thomas Hobbes abstracted the "sovereign" from the monarch, Jean-Jacques Rousseau identified the sovereign with the "will of the people," and John Locke lodged popular sovereignty in the lawmaking bodies and, therefore, primarily in the legislature. Constitutions put major emphasis on prescribing the legislative process. Since the objective of preventing the emergence of a despotic sovereign—whether ancien régime monarch, tyrannical majority, or totalitarian dictator—was at the center of liberal thought, the decision-making process acquired "checks and balances," requiring the cooperation of several institutions, adapting Montesquieu's interpretation of English government as separation of powers, and adopting limits on state authority in the form of rights. This established a model of legislative–executive decision making that became canonical, beginning with the Glorious Revolution (1688) in Great Britain and perpetuated in the United States Constitution (1789) and through it to many others. The rise and dramatic elaboration of the state apparatus with Napoleon's reforms and the German *Staat* did not change the institutions that shape the decision-making process. despite shifting much weight to the executive side. It did dramatically change the state apparatus itself, but that was considered to be "the administration," involved in applying the laws and policies, not deciding what they should be.

The nested models of representative government described in chapter 1 were based on the canonical model of decision making. The models seem to imply that identifying problems, setting agendas, and providing information about the real dimensions of a situation are components of the raw material fed into the legislative debate. Deputies, political parties, and interest groups link to the stakeholders. Giving voice to the preferences of sets of people is the main point of the models as I have drawn them. According to the deputy model, elected members of the legislature are the source of the information about their constituents' desires and needs. First political parties and then civil society associations and interest groups are added to the legislators in the partisan and pluralist models.

In these models, the interaction of these elements to make decisions was first institutionalized in debates in parliaments, and the legislative debate and vote became the penultimate step. Executive signature and promulgation became the final step, with the proviso that review by the judiciary or reconsideration by the legislature was a possibility.

The assumption of the models is that the core location of the decision-making process is in the last steps of the lawmaking process: the introduction, debate, vote, and passage of laws in the legislature and its negotiation with the executive. All the models suggest that a multitude of pressures, myriad demands, and much information come from outside the legislative process, but reconciling differences in interests or moral judgments, evaluating evidence from different sources, and factoring in predictions of the consequences of this or that policy choice are undertaken in those key, final stages.

As for what happens when these actors come together—what decision making is, in fact—the models are much less explicit. One typical perspective is an updated and pluralized version of the notion of decision making in the mind of a leader. When the representatives meet, they exercise their rhetorical skills in presenting their views, debate the issues, and come to a resolution.[1] In some fashion, not spelled out, a consensus or a majority opinion will emerge, most likely by means of a vote. Another very influential image of what making decisions entails is that it is essentially a type of bargaining. Since the deputies (or parties or interest groups) are defined by the interests of their "constituencies," the common assumption, patterned on the idea of the market, is that the debate in the legislature is, in fact, driven by a clash of interests. The means of resolving differences and finding an outcome that is satisfactory to all is negotiation. The ideal result is some sort of mutually acceptable compromise, involving "splitting the difference" or trading a loss in one area for a gain in another. The conventional understanding of politics and what makes it democratic is shaped by this image of a process of interest bargaining, leading to laws proclaimed by a single sovereign authority. The deputy, partisan, and pluralist models of institutions are varying conceptualizations of this process, indicating how interests are channeled into the legislative system and how the rhetorical jousting and hard bargaining are organized.

The two political facts that I discuss in the next two chapters raise questions about this way of defining the institutions and thus their reform. They challenge two assumptions made in the canonical view of the decision-making process.

The first assumption is that decision making is a matter of negotiation among those with competing interests or principles, not a deliberative process. Deliberation introduces cognitive elements into a policy discussion and has the potential—almost the certainty—to change the issue, the stakeholders, and the significance of any particular outcome. The inclusion of deliberation forces a radical new look at institutions that were imagined to handle bargaining.

The second assumption is that decision making is a single process. Especially in making policy rather than law, the legislature is not the only or even the principal venue in which reform is important. There are a great variety of channels to both legal and policy decisions. Institutions that regulate how these conduits are constructed (and adapted or dissolved) are the new targets of reform.

9

DELIBERATION IS
AS IMPORTANT AS
BARGAINING

*The way in which facts, theories, and interpretations are considered and shaped in
decision making affects the effectiveness and justice of decisions.*

Fact 5

The fifth fact that should change our conceptualization of representative institutions is a readily acknowledged truth about decision making: decision makers must process and evaluate information and ideas as well as preferences in order to make choices about policies and laws. It is a commonplace, but its relation to the problems of structuring a democratic political system demands more attention.

When any group of people collectively decide to do something—whether to establish standards they will live by or use their collective resources to act in some way—they have to resolve conflicts among themselves about what is the right thing and how to allocate benefits and costs. But they also must resolve uncertainties about the situation they face, the values at stake, the choices they have, and the consequences of various actions.

To write (or not write) a law that would decriminalize mind-altering drugs, for example, decision makers have to know about the moral debates about drugs as well as the stakes of legalization for drug dealers, law-enforcement officers, drug users, health officials, and pharmaceutical companies. But in addition to this information, they must know the facts about who is using the drugs, the likely impact of legalization on the market and on drug addiction, the ability of companies and pharmacies to supply users safely, the likely impact of decriminalization on the flow of illegal money to drug gangs, and the importance of this issue in relation to other concerns, such as the effect of drug-gang violence on democratic government in Mexico.

The information used is not simply a commodity obtained from a library, a Web site, or experts. It is the subject and output of a complex process of interaction with researchers, stakeholders, observers, and experienced administrators. This is a normal part of decision making. The information utilized in a debate is subject to elaboration, critical evaluation, obfuscation, and distortion. It evolves as a result of discussions, debates, arguments about its validity, about whether it supports the analysis of causes and consequences of choices, and about whether the values alleged to be affected are the most important. The discussions continue between experts (or those with the reputation for it), with those who have experience in writing and implementing policy (remembered accurately or not), and with the stakeholders who know (or think they know) what will affect them. In the course of discussion and debate, a process leads the parties to decide what will be taken as valid data, theories, and interpretations.[1]

This is the process that many refer to as "deliberation." It is a part of every decision and is often as important for the outcomes as is the resolution of disputes about the morally right course of action or the strategic games that determine who gets the benefits from the outcomes. It is the interaction of people involved in the decision around cognitive issues of data, theories, and interpretations, which can be analytically separated from bargaining over interests or confrontations over moral choices.[2]

Simplifying heroically, these are the three sorts of conflicts and uncertainties in political decision making, and therefore they indicate three sorts of processes to resolve or bypass them: negotiation among competing interests, choice among competing moral positions, and research and discussion to shape the cognitive elements of the decision. They differ in the competing elements, the process of interaction and the range of outcomes. To give them names, they are bargaining, moral argument, and deliberation.

• Bargaining between groups with competing claims on scarce resources is often considered to be the dominant process behind legal and policy decisions.[3] It is argued that the essence of the political process is who gets what, when, and how[4] and that the controlling process is a series of strategic choices made by representatives of groups working to maximize their interests through negotiation, trade-offs, compromise, or the exercise of power in favor of their own interests.

• Moral argument is also thought of as archetypically "political." Should we legalize abortion or gay marriage? Do we have the right or duty to overthrow dictators who are a threat to their own people and others? Should the state try to convert others to the true faith? Is the capitalist system or big government fundamentally evil? The divergent views may be about specific moral or religious question, or may escalate to a clash between different worldviews. Such questions are not often included in comparisons with deliberation and bargaining, since, perhaps, many observers think that moral choice is rational, while others believe that it is merely a preference and therefore a kind of interest. I think, however, that it deserves a separate category because of the distinct methods used in moral argument. The processes of coming to a collective decision (or agreement to disagree) on moral issues are quite different from those involved in bargaining and deliberation, and they may involve shaming, intimidating, exposing, or conversion. As is very apparent in the world today, moral argument has a serious potential for violent imposition or nihilist destruction. Indeed, the justification for violence is often rooted in intractable moral positions.

• Deliberation involves the provision of information and the collective processing of that information into law and policy.

Problems that demand political decisions always involve all three aspects of decision making, although often the central issue, the major conflict, is over one of them: interests, moral positions, or facts. Deliberation may be overshadowed (or taken over) by one or both of the other processes, but it is always there and is capable of having an independent impact. Debate over the facts, the explanations, and the interpretations may be undertaken to support a moral position or buttress claims on behalf of an interest, but often is much closer to the center of the process. For example, in decisions about dealing with a natural disaster, such as the earthquake and tsunami in Japan, interests came into play and moral questions involved with blame were important, but the central questions that demanded immediate attention were those of fact and the accuracy of theories about the causes of the "meltdown" of nuclear reactors. The problems of public debt, financial instability, and long-term unemployment, which dominate the news in the midst of an economic recession, engage class interests and the morality of taxes and government action, but at the center are factual questions: Why did it happen? What measures would get us out of it? The availability of information—data, theories, and interpretations—to answer such questions is, in this digital age, enormous. More complicated to assess are the mechanisms to evaluate, refine, and bring information to bear on a decision.

Facts are not simply facts. The public media deluges us with "facts" presented by those with potentially hidden agendas, with what might be called the "advertising mentality." Lying and making up facts may not happen as often as cynics allege, but a strong selection process is to be expected that shapes and limits information. The range of lobbyists is so wide that there must be great variation on the scale of "serious presentation of facts" to "hyperbole on behalf of the client." The activities of research organizations and academic centers, public and private policy shops, are influenced by their own professional ethics and by their consumers—the decision makers—to some standard of checking and evaluating information. Fact checking and theory testing—all techniques well developed for some purposes—may or may not be applied to policy making.

Explanations about the consequences of past choices and potential future ones are central to the task of choosing policies or laws. Conventional wisdom and professional literature offer many reasons for the fall of trade between two countries, the subtle changes in climate and their consequences, the inclination of some teenagers to become terrorists, the chance that Iran will build an atomic bomb, the increase of teenage pregnancy among certain groups, and so forth. In most cases, there are means to test the hypotheses offered, but they are not always built into the process of decision making.

Interpretations of what values are engaged by a problem and how they relate to other actions or ideals of a community are also easy to find in this digital age. Pundits and bloggers, commentators and imams, critical observers and movement activists have much access to the public and to the decision makers. The process of distinguishing the sensational from the serious, the perceptive from the "knee-jerk" is not simple. Filtering the cacophony is difficult, but must be done to guide decision makers.

It is not only the supply of information that counts, but the way the interaction and treatment of that information—that is, the actual deliberation—

takes place. There are many forms: discussions, dialogues, confrontations, meetings in secret between publicly hostile leaders, committee discussions after hearings, and conferences, to name a few. It even goes on to some extent in public debates in legislatures, blogs, and television shows—although most legislators, bloggers, and commentators use the opportunity to present their points of view, not to engage with (except, perhaps, to overpower), those with opposing perspectives.

It is a complex process to introduce information into the decision-making process, compare it with other information, weigh the relative merits of alternatives, and work out conclusions.[5] Deliberation does not go on only in the heads of the decision makers after being exposed to the information in the press and reports from research organizations. It is a process of give-and-take, evaluation, and discussion. Concrete deliberations may take place among members of a group of high-level decision makers, but the chances are great that on any but the simplest issue, they will hold hearings, convene conferences, or conduct extended interviews in which experts are invited to present their (often conflicting) views. Such experts may be officials with practical experience in carrying out policy or the clarity from knowing that they will be responsible for doing so, people familiar with "best practices" in other countries, scholars who have done research on the question, people who have been affected by earlier efforts, and officials informed about financial and other resources.

The decision made by the Bush administration to invade Iraq is best understood, I believe, as a failure of deliberation. Not only was the data about weapons of mass destruction faulty, but the understanding of the consequences of an invasion—even a slam-dunk "conquest"—was significantly off the mark. Many critics assumed that the decision was a case of the pursuit of special interests and blamed the oil companies allied with George W. Bush. Alternatively, they considered it a question of imposing a moral judgment shaped by the mind-set of Bush's entourage about Arabs and Muslims and shaped by the earlier "failure" of Bush's father to topple Saddam Hussein. However much either of these reasons might explain the choice made, the disastrous decision had a lot to do with the failure to understand what it meant to invade a country as a way to deal with the terrorism of September 11—particularly a country not involved in the attacks.

If it is accepted that the United States went to war because of serious errors of fact and theory, it is not enough to say that members of the Bush administration were wrong, ignorant, or willfully misrepresenting the facts and leave it there. Norms, or even laws, mandating an effort to correct them should have been in place. The process of deliberation—processing information, talking it out, meeting objections, checking facts, refining theories—took place only within a narrow group and brought in contrary evaluations and arguments too late to affect the decision. It is the absence of serious deliberation that has to be singled out as problematic, not any one group's state of mind.

Another example of the introduction of cognitive elements into a decision that has material and moral dimensions can be found when a state (say, Mexico) is confronted with the problem of how to deal with a powerful neighbor (say, the United States) that wants to implement or strengthen free-trade policies. The process of making a decision in Mexico no doubt will involve bargaining among established interests with material stakes in the outcome. Manufacturers of goods will face new, serious competition; financial sectors will have investment opportunities, but new rivals; labor unions will have the chance for new organization, but may lose established gains. These interests and many others will stand to gain by placating the neighbor or will secure useful political support from forces that oppose it. The process of deciding whether to cooperate with or resist the neighbor and how to do so, to be sure, has a strong bargaining element.

Moral choices will no doubt be posed, too. Some may reject the neighbor state on the grounds of its culpability for past sins of imposition. Others may feel that the principle of free trade must be adhered to, even (or especially) in the face of uncertainty of its short-term effects, having faith that in the long run it must be better for all. Still others, conversely, may see the reduction of barriers as a path to cultural deterioration or corruption of their society, as it opens its border to bad influences in drugs, consumerism, or militarism. The adoption of one or another course of action may involve choosing among these values or compromising them. The process of decision will be shaped in part by the confrontation of these positions in the legislature and in the cabinet, on the street and in the media.

But the deliberative element may be as important as or even more crucial than the material and moral factors. A great deal of the action on an issue like this involves marshaling evidence, explanations, and interpretations of what is going on, and then arguing, debating, and engaging in a dialogue about them. The participants in the process of adopting a trade policy will show how the evidence demonstrates why one or another policy or (more likely) variation on the proposals will be good or bad for particular interests or for the country—increasing growth and rationalizing production, on the one hand, and generating unemployment and causing displacement on the other. The evidence will be statistical records, supported by what will be claimed to be reputable theory that shows that the statistics are connected to overall growth rates and prosperity. The challenges to the evidence will question its meaning: whether the problem has been formulated correctly, whether the measures used are appropriate, and whether the conclusions are justified.

Deliberation takes place in earnest when the information has been presented and the actors are engaged in dialogue: trading ideas; convincing others or agreeing to disagree temporarily; reaching consensus on a tentative plan; and, perhaps, deciding to look at the results later and reconsider if necessary.

If nothing else happened other than the mobilization of experts by each side, the process might be only bargaining. Sometimes the ideas and evidence presented are essentially just rationalizations and screens to promote or perhaps even obfuscate the issues on behalf of the major stakeholders, rather than an effort to get at a more adequate understanding of a situation. The businesses in favor of free trade hire their own economists, as do the unions representing workers in companies that cannot survive the competition that will result from free trade. It is possible that so little value is placed on the information that no deliberation takes place. Reducing the debate to a choice between competing sets of facts, theories, and interpretations that support competing interests is not deliberation.

A stylized version of the adversarial legal procedure is a model that seems to encourage a view of decision making as a choice between competing partisan presentations of information. The prosecution and the defense bring their own experts. The processes of deliberation—deciding between prosecution and defense—take place in the mind of the judge and/or the jury members. In the case of a political decision, the judge and jury might be the supreme leader—a version of autocratic rule. Alternatively, the public at large deliberates while deciding on their votes or, more diffusely, when their judgment is tapped by opinion polling. Both letting the king do it and letting the public decide are methods of minimally organized deliberation. Both are of doubtful effectiveness in either making a decision adequate to solve complex problems or making any decision at all.

Deliberation takes place all the time, if not always well. All systems have significant numbers of decision makers at all levels who are open to changing their minds on the basis of new facts, new theories, or new ways of thinking about problems. The incentive to develop new information may come from the desire to enhance one's material or moral position, but the process of deliberation has an independent share in determining the outcomes.

Data, theories, and interpretations are readily available, and debating processes are found in many locations. Government officials may form a commission or a study group to reconcile the theories, offer new ones, adduce new evidence, or produce a new interpretation that reconceptualizes a problem. Serious dialogues take place in universities and research centers, sometimes with international input, and the print and broadcast media generate their own discussions with "public intellectuals" and columnists. And, increasingly, the Internet becomes engaged, with discussion forums and blogs providing channels to offer and debate information. In one fashion or another the process of clarifying the uncertainties may escape the control of the groups and individuals who had the initial stake in the process.

DELIBERATION AND THE CLASSIC MODELS
OF REPRESENTATION

Addressing the question of institutional reform requires identifying the processes of deliberation that may be controlled by sets of rules and norms— that is, institutions. The classic models of the institutions of representative government, which I have described as the deputy, partisan, and pluralist models, contain elements of deliberation, but often hidden behind various assumptions.

• The most common model of deliberation in democratic politics is, of course, the activity of the legislature, often referred to as the deliberative body. It is at the core of the deputy model, among others. The sovereignty of the legislature over the executive was one of the triumphs of the liberal vision in the American and French constitutions and the later ones modeled on them.[6] The template for these legislative bodies were the councils and parliaments, the talking shops of the old regime. Although emperors and kings depended first on the advice of a few trusted advisers, the need to call a council—in France, the Estates General—to debate and agree on the resources the king needed, usually to conduct wars, was a prelude to the evolution of the sovereign legislature. A debating and advising club became the central point of the challenge to the authority of the king.

Along with the interest representation and moral posturing to be expected from deputies identified with regional or class interests in the legislature are the application of knowledge and use of debates to clarify issues in lawmaking. In some eras, the relevant facts, theories, and interpretations were generally assumed to be part of the equipment of those who were sent to parliamentary meetings, and, ideally, deliberation took the form of conversations among gentlemen. With the complications of new knowledge, novel problems, and more complex questions, legislators utilized their personal connections, acquired staffs, established committees, and convened hearings. The information is brought by the deputies, and the debates and committee meetings in which it is evaluated and presumably improved are built into the legislature, as is the mechanism for making a final determination—usually some sequence of agreements or votes.

As issues change and new sources of information become available, the assumption is that legislators themselves will adapt their roles appropriately. In the purest form of the liberal version of the deputy model, the only appropriate legal framework to be established is the guarantee of freedom of speech. The free market of ideas will take care of the rest. But it was probably always the case that rules for committees, hearings, and public and closed discussions were, in fact, institutions that shaped deliberation. Whether they promoted the people's interests is not certain.

• The partisan model brings a different sense of deliberation to the polity. In their early form as factions at court, political parties were likely to be personal followings of a powerful courtier. Even at this stage, they represented a form of structuring debate. With the rise of the legislature, they took on a more important role, which they often still have: formulating the contrasting positions that constitute the "sides" in a debate. They sometimes are impelled, in fact, to create these contrasts, since the institution of competitive elections supports and reinforces the distinctions between parties. As broad principles were shaped by one or more "sides," the deliberation became a confrontation among broad principles. Probably the first partisan bodies that pushed this confrontational style were religious, but it became explicitly articulated in the period identified with Karl Marx. Political parties made claims to comprehensively organize the provision of information and the progress of debate. This process, in the classic Marxist form (and current American super-partisan politics), is thought of more as a confrontation than a deliberation in the legislature and the press. The point is not to convince, but to win the right to impose their solution. And winning requires mobilizing supporters, not persuading opponents, so deliberation takes place mainly within the party.

In a strong partisan model, the debate is first about the principles of a program. In some cases, most strikingly in the "democratic centralist" periods of Communist practice, the program is taken as a given, explicated by the leading members of the party. The partisan system may embrace an active deliberation among the leading members of each party about the "line" to be taken in the confrontation with competing parties. In this hard-line version of the partisan model, the crucial step of convincing people is the effort to mobilize those who, by the principles espoused, ought to adhere to them.

The espousal of "programs" and "platforms" in current political rhetoric reveals the continuing attractiveness of this hard-line image of the role of political parties in the shaping of political discourse, even after the comprehensive retreat from broad, "ideological" tenets. Parties are supposed to have "principles" that they defend. A certain part of the public media can become involved in a broad discussion of these principles, but the main significance is to appeal to a grievance, not to promote discussion. They may be seen, however, as shaping the deliberative process to the extent that when a party wins an election, it installs its "team" in the leading administrative and legislative posts, and debate over policy is carried out among the members of the inner circle. The most salient deliberative qualities of the partisan model are presumably the election campaigns that bring a party to power. It should be clear from recent American experience that the election campaign confrontation between parties—however many "debates" among candidates, dueling talk shows, and competing television stations—is a very blunt instrument for creating the dialogue about the information that is key to decision making. The potential for serious deliberation between political parties is obviously present, but the institutions for implementing it are not in place and may never be.[7]

• The pluralist model—despite its history of being focused around the promotion of particular interests, and therefore being more suited to the bargaining image of politics than the deliberative one—can be thought of as one response to the weakening of political parties in institutionalizing deliberation, at least in the provision-of-information phase. Any study of policy making includes references to the way in which interest groups or groups of concerned citizens (or any of the many ways that civil society associations present themselves) provide legislators, political leaders, and administrative officials with information. Such information is not only factual, about the desires of the special interests, but also interpretations of polls, results of scientific experiments, and opinions of experts. The pluralist model provides a distinctive way to show the rich sources of information that feed into the deliberative process.

In the processing of information, however, classic versions of the pluralist model do not suggest a strong role for interest groups in contributing to deliberation. As lobbyists, they are regarded as being engaged in a sales pitch. Like the ubiquitous advertisements inducing potential consumers to buy, lobbyists are seen as interested only in gaining support, not in winning arguments. Convincing a legislator or an official of the validity of the information presented no doubt involves interactions, but there is normally little back-and-forth discussion, debate, or adjustment of opinions and judgments—in other words, deliberation. In the pluralist model, deliberation takes place either in the minds of decision makers or among legislators. In the social-movement version of the model, deliberation takes place in the movement or in the government's effort to find a formula to mollify the activists.

THE CHALLENGES OF DELIBERATION HAVE DEMOCRATIC OUTCOMES

Deliberation is not a goal, but a fact. Although the traditional models of representative institutions speak to various elements of deliberation, they do not incorporate the most active sites where deliberation plays a central role, such as the opinion and argumentative side of the media, academia, research centers, and the myriad staff meetings, conferences, and working-group sessions held to "thrash out" ideas. These are the constitutive elements of deliberative arenas, or "public spheres."[8] The models also do not provide guidance about the regulation of deliberation being done in these venues to improve the efficiency and justice of the decisions.

Because of its focus on problems, deliberation poses another hurdle for reform: the need to adjust the process to new situations. Institutionalizing deliberative processes cannot be done at a "constitutional" moment and then left. It has to be a continuing project, with norms for building venues for deliberation, not just for operating them. They often have to be constructed anew or modified if a different set of interests is engaged, a different set of stakeholders, a new technology, or new insights. Think of the impact of the discovery and mapping of the human genome on the way in which many parts of medicine and thus health-care policy are conceived.

An issue may emerge because of a crisis, a conflict among major interests, or a moral challenge. The system, so to speak, must search for the right set of people and links and decision makers to address the new situation. A novel process of information gathering and deliberation will have to develop: finding relevant facts and theories, presenting new or modified explanations, and offering new interpretations of the significance of the issue for consideration.

Some common assumptions seem to imply that a new issue does not cause great change in the deliberative process. That might be true if "experts" were one group of people, such as the gentlemen representatives in early legislatures were assumed to be. Setting up appropriate sources of information might not be complicated if the stakeholders could be classified in groups that encompassed all issues: proletariat or bourgeoisie, those for or against big government and taxes, nationalists or anti-nationalists, believers or nonbelievers. Then the only problem would be to find the appropriate interpreter of the faith. But stakeholders are not homogeneous, and a more fundamental reorganization of the deliberative process has to take place if it is to produce decisions in the interests of the people as they actually are. Information about and the appropriate group to discuss the dynamics of migration of Muslims to France will not be the same as those for questions about the future of French viniculture. The identification of new stakeholders—and therefore new participants, new sets of information, and ultimately new ways of deliberating about the issue—does not happen infrequently.

The deliberative process itself is a source of change. Indeed, if it is working, it is one of the main sources of change. People are not infrequently "redefined" in the course of policy deliberation. This is not a question of someone becoming "someone else"—getting married, emigrating, growing older, getting a middle-class job—but of being redefined because an issue is reinterpreted, reconceptualized, which changes the stakes involved.

Sometimes the process is slow. For example, parts of the marginal, illegal street businesses in the cities of developing countries were transformed in self-image and others' perceptions into components of the "informal economy." From being a problem of law and order, they became a potentially significant source of productivity and innovation.[9] Some of the vendors were redefined as entrepreneurs operating with minimal resources, even though they continued for a while to be harassed and constrained by the government's regulations and law enforcement. Not all of them were so redefined. Some elements in the marginal sectors became identified as contributors to the international drug trade, and others remained simply the intractably poor. The different segments of these "marginal" populations were seen to have very different interests and had to be brought into the representative system in different ways. Sociological and economic changes were involved, but the transformation had most to do with new insights about economic development.

The redefinition of "marginals" took place over perhaps a decade. Another example shows a more rapid change and the problems of misperception. The decision of the United States to invade two countries, Afghanistan and Iraq, as a way to counter the threat from terrorists implied a new set of theories (or the resurrection of old ones) that all security threats were derived from nation-states—which, in this case, were thought to have purposely harbored the terrorists responsible for the attacks on September 11. It seemed plausible to argue that the Islamic fundamentalist terrorists were state actors, rather than sectarian marginals. The deliberation on this issue—which did not take place at the time of the decision—slowly discovered the weakness of this analysis, and the problem changed.

Another example arises during the adoption of free trade in a country less powerful than its neighbor, as mentioned earlier. Multiple group interests are involved, but over time the issue may evolve from being about free trade between the two countries to being about managing labor flows or dealing with environmental threats or global geopolitical realignments. Workers in the country being asked to accept free trade may separate into various groups, depending on their relationship to the new definition of the issue and the new evidence about the impacts of various policies. When the debate shifts from the protection of national businesses from international competition to a theory of development in "global" terms, "labor" ceases to be a cohesive nationalist group and is divided between workers who would benefit from the new factories and those who would be isolated because of inefficiency. "Business" also fragments, depending on how companies may adapt to international competition. This is not a question of bargaining or, despite the rhetoric, moral positions, but of a transformation in the way of looking at the problem and an awareness of real changes in economic factors like transportation and skills that alter the interest identities of many people.[10]

There are other reasons why the panoply of interests change, including a burst of new immigration, economic collapse, and a threat of war. And some cognitive changes are merely the recognition of such dislocations. The cognitive aspects of deliberation are not alone in making adaptation necessary. But in all cases of changing definitions and divisions of stakeholders, ways of formulating the challenges, understandings of the conditions that shape the goals and how to achieve them, and patterns of information retrieval and deliberation about that information must evolve. If we could rely on the "aristocrats" of the legislature to adapt on the basis of their intelligence and flexibility (which does happen, of course), there would be no problem. But during the process of decision making, actors not only build networks among officials, but often create a set of organizations, networks, meetings, and committees that stretch into the civil society. In that case, the norms, rules, and laws that shape the deliberative process must adapt as well.

The fact is that the outcome of political decision making is heavily influenced by the introduction of and dialogue about facts setting out the situation, theories showing how things work and consequences of contemplated action, and interpretations of their significance. This deliberation defines the stakeholders and may lead to changes in their identity. It provides the knowledge that gives reason to policy and law. Moral principles may trump instrumental concerns, but even that requires deliberation to specify the costs. The actual deliberation that goes on does not by any means always lead to optimal outcomes for the people. It may go bad. If special interests seize control of the deliberative process, it may yield policies and laws that serve only their interests. If a group with total faith in its own vision of the world prevents open, serious discussion, the political outcomes may be distorted. If the process relies on faulty data, erroneous theories, or misleading interpretations—which no amount of discussion can correct—the outcome may be bad through no one's fault, except the imperfect science that went into it. Deliberation is a vital part of democratic legislation and policy making. Reforming democracies without shaping how it is done is likely to fail.

10

DECISIONS ARE MADE
IN MULTIPLE VENUES

Decisions are made in various venues, not just the legislature, and how those venues operate and interact affects whether the outcomes are effective and just.

Fact 6

I have already alluded to the reality of multiple and evolving decision networks, spaces, and procedures. They arise from the shifting sets of citizens and quasi-citizens, the initiatives taken through transitory personal networks, the constantly reconfiguring civil society associations, and the changing definitions of problems. A common assumption is that all these networks feed their information and conclusions into a final process: the legislative-plus-executive final decision procedure. The result of the actions in these networks is only to influence the debate in the final stage. That, it is assumed, is where the "real action" takes place.

This is partly right, mostly wrong. If "real action" means putting the decision into effect as a law, then the assumption is correct in the sense that the formal promulgation and recognition of laws is the endpoint of the legislative process. Even with respect to officially sanctioned rules, though, many executive decrees and regulations are decisions that escape the legislature altogether. Much more relevant for democracy is that the last step of putting the decision into effect as a law is often a registration of decisions made elsewhere. The "real action" for assessing the sources of the welfare of the people is deliberation, moral argument, and bargaining—that is, decision making. These processes often take place outside formal legislative proceedings. On a few issues, particularly those that do not lead to a partisan standoff, the legislature may be the locus of serious debate and negotiation. Usually, legislatures either simply ratify deals made elsewhere or showcase differences between the parties for electoral or other public-relations reasons. If we are interested in the institutions that shape outcomes, we must look where the decisions are shaped, and not just where the final legal products are incorporated into the standing laws of the country. We are interested in where decision making actually takes place, not where it is supposed to. The actual deliberation, moral argument, and bargaining are conducted in many venues of various kinds.[1] They cannot be summarized in a few lines of constitutional prose. That multiplicity is the sixth political fact, which, I argue, requires rethinking in the agenda for reform.

FEDERAL SYSTEMS, REGIONAL INTEGRATION, AND AUTONOMOUS AGENCIES

To have a multiplicity of decision-making venues may seem chaotic, but some arenas beyond the standard ones are well recognized, ordered, and institutionalized. Chapter 4 considers the challenges of making decisions in federal systems and supranational entities, which entails building links among multiple governments and dealing with quasi-citizens. Here I wish to point to the way that in those clusters of systems, separate decision-making processes coexist and often are regulated by constitutional or treaty language. In federal systems, the governments of the subordinate jurisdictions (states, provinces) are given responsibility for decision making on a certain range of issues. The division of authority in federal systems is set out in constitutions, and courts have the power to arbitrate between the central and subordinate jurisdictions. Specifying just how decision making is carried out in those units is as complicated as it is for the central government. But they are different venues, and it is understood that part of shaping a democratic system is improving the decision-making processes at both levels.[2]

Separate decision-making processes are established for both the superior and subordinate units. From the point of view of a particular state or province, many laws and policies relevant to it are decided by means of a process that takes place (and claims authority) over it (and usually other states and provinces) but is not within its territory. When a set of political units build a new authority over themselves from "below" they are establishing a new decision-making process that will have some measure of authority over them.

The formation of the United States was classic, and led to the founding of a strong country that rivaled the nation-states of Europe. American federal authority is still contested, but in any case it established and institutionalized very extensive power over the briefly sovereign colonial states.

In the wake of the world wars in the twentieth century, there were efforts to build a global federal state; but rather than create a state-like sovereign authority, councils were created that could act basically if there was universal consensus among the heads of state. Nevertheless, a variety of international agencies—such as the International Labor Organization, World Health Organization, High Commission for Human Rights, and United Nations Educational, Scientific, and Cultural Organization—became the source of decisions, quasi-laws and policies. They were established not on the model of the United States, under a single authoritative lawmaking power (although they are nominally responsible to the General Assembly), but like an administrative structure of a nation without the conventional apparatus of sovereign lawmaking over them. The broadly perceived need for international regulation and policies on labor practices, disease control, migration, protection of minorities, and law enforcement, among other concerns, has pushed the decision-making structures to go beyond the heads of states and toward incorporating interest groups, professional associations, international activists, and many other stakeholders into their decision-making processes. Their democratic qualities (which most observers would accept) come not from a formal electoral or legislative process, in the manner of the conventional models of representative democracy, but through the links that separate agencies establish with the people. For most countries, they are separate decision-making venues that have plausible authority in the countries' territory.[3]

For the past half century, the European Union has been forming from the semi-integration of the countries that centuries ago pioneered as independent, sovereign nation-states. The EU has shaped many pieces of a federal system, creating commissions, a parliament, and bureaucracies. The establishment of authoritative regulatory or lawmaking bodies has raised many questions about "democratic deficits" and effectiveness. The process of deciding how to judge their democratic qualities and what reforms would enhance them is still very much under way.[4]

Another set of examples of relatively well-established, separate decision-making venues for a political system are the autonomous agencies of government found in many countries. They are, like subordinate jurisdictions in federal systems, relatively well-institutionalized forms with varying degrees of independence from the national law- and policy-making processes. Central banks, housing authorities, public-land commissions, regulatory agencies, and many others are insulated from the decision-making processes of the legislature and executive to free them from short-term "political" influences and allow them to discuss, bargain, and decide about many aspects of, for example, monetary policy, transportation safety, and health regulations.

The autonomy of such agencies is, of course, relative. The legal framework that protects them from "politics" takes many forms and works in different ways. But as with any "independent" body, their decisions can be overturned by a determined executive or be undercut by local and international agencies. Their decisions are not free from influences from society, not only domestic but international. But the conscious effort is to make them at least semi-autonomous.

However independent they are, making the arrangement a part of representative government presents problems. The organization of autonomous agencies themselves raises the usual question about the balance of stakeholders and neutral parties. Should central banks be run by bankers? The involvement of experts becomes crucial to ensure a sophisticated understanding of financial information. Should economists from academia be included? How should the interests of the poor, whose lives will no doubt be affected by economic decisions, be represented? Beyond the internal structure are questions about how the agencies fit into the larger policy-making system: On what range of issues are they the final decision makers? What powers do they have over the national administration? What authority do they have to punish those who violate their directives?

Questions like these are posed almost automatically with the establishment of an autonomous agency, and in established democratic systems the rules about how and within what limits they are to function are usually defined, although concerns persist about whether and how these rules promote the welfare of the whole people as opposed to the interests of the group being regulated. What makes central banks take action for the people and not just for the banks? What makes drug regulatory agencies set standards to benefit the people and not only for the pharmaceutical industry or the medical profession?

The institutionalization of the rules that regulate autonomous agencies is complicated by the fact that noncitizens play an important and necessary role in the decisions made by many of them, and these decisions have important consequences in other jurisdictions. The role of central banks is tied closely to the international economic system: other central banks, international financial institutions, and "too big to fail" international businesses, trading organizations, and the like. Since the decisions about credit or monetary policies have an impact on countries other than that in which the bank is chartered and rely on the reactions in those countries to be effective, the decision-making structure has to find ways of discovering the conditions and likely responses in those countries, even if the primary concern of a central bank is the core citizenry of the country that established it.

Writing the rules that regulate these agencies requires that attention be paid to the continually changing character of their tasks. The challenges for central banks are constantly being revised, with new forms of economic crises, new technologies, and new world trade configurations. The changes present not only a new context for dealing with the same people, but new sets of people. What entities or laws manage the creation or modification of decision-making patterns to deal with new situations? Major consequences for the effectiveness and justice of a central bank's policies will flow from the way it responds to, say, the rise of China as a major economic power. The central bankers will no doubt set up consultations with experts on the Chinese economy, rearrange links with financial firms, and build new ties to international negotiators.

Exploring the rules that would make the interplay of these separate decision-making processes more likely to be democratic and work in the public interest is an important topic. A less often visited problem is the decision-making venues that do not have the autonomous agencies' level of constitutional regulation.

DECISION NETWORKS

Much of the "real action" of making political decisions—the linking with citizens and quasi-citizens, the confrontation of interests; the debates over the rightness of laws and policies; the gathering, evaluating, and processing of information—is done by an ad hoc network of stakeholders, advisers, and decision makers.[5] These networks do not have the authority to independently make laws, but feed into the last steps of law- and/or policy making: chief executive signature, promulgation of laws, proclamation of executive decrees, or authoritative commitment of resources. They are networks whose roots are working groups, personal connections, "neo-corporatist" links, and many other sources.

I call them "decision networks." They are composed of people and organizations that are linked together; have procedures to discuss, debate, bargain, argue, and offer solutions to particular problems; and enjoy direct access to the final step of legal promulgation or executive decree proclamation. Without these two features—the means of deliberation, moral argument, and bargaining *and* the entrée to an authoritative promulgator—they would not be relevant here. Without a decision-making process, they would be showcases for opinions (as are most blogs). Without access to power, they would be talking shops. Both opinion showcases and talking shops are useful for many things—educating the public, thinking innovatively about emerging challenges, generating new personal links—but it is the networks with both decision-making capabilities and access to power that are the crucial ones for democracy.

Decision networks are created or form on their own for many reasons. There may be a need to link expertise with experience. Measures to deal with climate change, to support research on renewable sources of energy, and to deliver medical care to poor children may lead to meetings with knowledgeable scientists, practitioners, and policy specialists. Sometimes open media or public discussions on issues like abortion and the status of women are threatened by showcase violence or disruption, and serious representatives of the various positions will be brought together in a more insulated group. Whether because of the sensitivity of a topic, the need to work through complex data, or the crassness of the deals that have to be made, it is often much easier and more rational to delegate the hard choices to a special decision network created for the purpose than to try to debate in the formalized setting of a legislature or a "town-hall meeting."

Some networks are called into being by officials or legislators. Perhaps a decision requires compromise on moral positions that officials do not want to do in public. Perhaps the tangle of issues is too complex for legislators to deal with in open debate (which they are not very good at doing) or for officials in the executive branch to handle expeditiously. Perhaps a decision is needed quickly, and a working group is a shortcut around the established procedures. If a decision requires a realization in law, the fact of a prior agreement may make its transit through the legislative process more rapid. If, as is increasingly the case, the decision requires the collaboration and compliance of foreign governments or foreign businesses, a working group may be the only way to bring them together.[6]

Decision networks are often, but not always, temporary and issue-specific. They often are where the work of reviewing evidence, evaluating theories, consulting major stakeholders, and redefining or agreeing to disagree about moral stances takes place. Their output will almost always be subject to approval by some authority, but for a large number of complex or delicate problems, reopening the discussion is often too costly in time and/or politically dangerous, and thus the decisions they make are often almost final.

Decision-making processes that avoid these networks and go directly from a presentation by lobbyists, policy shops, or activists to a final discussion in a legislature are much rarer than the imagery of the representative models would have us believe. It is a commonplace that deals are often "cut in the back room," although that phrase implies a negative judgment of the process, which is by no means always justified. It is no surprise that in order to resolve a conflict between the political parties in the legislature, a president holds conferences with members of the contending parties, together with experts and observers, to arrive at a resolution.

Devices to bring a decision network into being have long been part of executive practice, in the form of "advisory" groups. They may be a cluster of trusted advisers of an executive: a "kitchen cabinet." They are an established part of legislatures, too, as standing and special committees with the power to hold hearings. The visible part of these formations is composed of perhaps only a handful of individuals. They deserve to be called "decision networks" because the members are picked for, are appointed to, or find their way into a group because of the network of friends and supporters of the executive or legislators, policy and legal experts, experienced practitioners in administering relevant policies, and savvy public-relations people. The working group is always a bundle of connections and links.

A working group may be (or later be seen as) a conspiracy of some stakeholders in the decision to be made who manage to get the ear of the "right people." It may be an investigative commission, formally established by the legislature or the executive to look into a problem, hear various policy and political experts and others who could be affected, and formulate a plan of action. It may be an informal group of members of different government agencies, linked by personal or professional ties, who come together to discuss and shape a common concern that may turn into a policy proposal. It may be a set of researchers brought together at a conference who articulate a new approach to health care, energy efficiency, or teenage pregnancy. It may be a network of economists and activists brought together by staff members of legislators to deal with joblessness. Although political figures have always been known for their "contacts," the availability of electronic media makes the construction of decision networks far easier and perhaps, not surely, more effective.[7]

However important the members and their links are for the law and policy outcomes, the manner in which groups conduct bargaining, moral argument, and deliberation is crucial as well. An open discussion may not produce a relevant decision because some members do not have the information about or understanding of the positions of other members. But, equally, a broadly representative set of members may not produce decisions that touch on all concerns because the discussion procedures are faulty. The outcomes will be determined as much by the way the interaction in the group takes place as by who has a seat at the table.

Progress in negotiating a workable bargain, transforming a conflict of opinion into a collective insight, or arriving at a working consensus (or an agreement to disagree) on moral issues constitute the core of the decision-making process, and they often take place in these networks.

THE SIGNIFICANCE OF DECISION NETWORKS
FOR DEMOCRACY

When decision networks are purely advisory—that is, only presenting proposals for the executive or legislature to review and arrive at its own decisions—the rules to make the process democratic are relatively straightforward. They may be limited to accountability. In the classic models, if the executive or legislators establish a commission, take its advice, and implement its proposals, the democratic "right thing to do" is to reward or punish the advisees at the polls—depending on the success or failure of the policy.

But, I am suggesting, a great deal of hard work goes into decision making by decision networks. If a group tackles a complicated issue, it is unlikely that the advisee has the time or capacity to review and weigh all the evidence, examine and assess the relevant theoretical literature, evaluate the moral questions involved, and consider the relative importance of the interests of various actors. He or she is more likely to count on the wisdom exercised in choosing a network's members and setting up the group's procedures. Taking its advice—perhaps with a slight variation to "put his or her stamp" on it—relies on the standards used. It is also unlikely that the presentation of the network's conclusions in the legislature will lead to a debate that will recapitulate or extend the group's work. If different commissions or decision networks come up with different positions, there will be a standoff or a new working group will be established.

When the executive or legislators take a working group's advice, which is much more likely than rethinking the issue, and the people do not like it, the standard method of achieving democracy is voting out or otherwise punishing the advisees. This is a very blunt instrument. To ensure that the output of this widely prevalent decision-making venue is likely to be favorable to the people's interests, it is necessary to establish principles for the creation and adaptation of decision networks.

Some think that groups of experts are always anti-democratic. Some consider these decision networks to be anathema from the standpoint of the public interest. In a manner parallel to the conventional views of personal networks as probably corrupt (as discussed in chapter 7), decision networks can be regarded as the antithesis of popular participation, which is often taken as the sine qua non of a democratic system. The assemblage of experts divorced from "everyman" or of stakeholders with special interests and the money to influence the discussion, as well as the relative privacy of the proceedings, which suggests something to hide, raise suspicion. And there is no question that all of these factors are possible and may produce nondemocratic results.

Whether or not the decision networks contribute to or detract from democracy depends on the links between a group and the stakeholders among the core and quasi-citizens. Since a network is likely to have a specialized task, the notion of special interests dominating its deliberations and influencing its proposals is not unwarranted. But whether these special interests override more public interest is an empirical question, not a necessary fact. It is precisely the construction and operation of and the patterns of access to the working group to which the idea of institutions—rules, regulations, practices—is important. The fact is that there are many venues of decision making, and the conventional institutions of representative democracy are not good at regulating them.[8] Institutions with a serious chance of promoting just and effective decisions have to adapt to the real pattern of decision making.[9]

Decision networks are a rational way to deal with the conditions of too little time, information "overload," and too many publicly held "unchangeable" moral commitments, as well as the need to include quasi-citizens with no status in the formal bodies of government. Thus they have become a frequently used decision-making venue, making "near final" decisions. The lesson must be, therefore, that the institutions—the laws, norms, and habits—of policy making must not work to eliminate them, but to shape, regulate, and optimize them. Institutional reform with the goal of improving the performance of a political system must, in other words, be addressed not simply to the legislative process (elections, lobbying, party systems, executive-legislative interactions) but at the multiplicity of decision-making venues—both formal ones in federal systems and independent agencies and informal ones in the clusters of decision networks that surround contemporary governments.

CONCLUSION

A REVIEW

The six facts about politics discussed in this book expose six false but common assumptions about the process of democratic representation. They point to complex social and political actions that escape the effective control of the institutions in the traditional models of representation discussed in chapter 1. Reforming the way in which deputies in a legislature relate to their constituents, elections are conducted, party systems operate, and interest groups lobby will never be an effective strategy of democratic reform without also paying attention to the processes discussed here. The activities that these six facts point to exist beside, beyond, and behind these now classic institutions, and reforming only the conventional institutions will not touch much of the real dynamics. The need is for new thinking about the rules and norms that govern this activity and the institutions that might be shaped to render them more democratic.

The facts I have discussed are common knowledge, but the common practice is to ignore them, to make assumptions that are known to be not completely true, but that simplify the analysis. Simplicity of theory is the soul of science, explaining phenomena that appear complex by means of elegantly simple propositions and formulas.[1] But that emphatically should not mean leaving out complicating factors rather absorbing them into more sophisticated concepts. Without such incorporation, simplification can become illegitimate reductionism and a recipe for failure.

My argument in this book is that we can no longer afford to treat these facts as troublesome details. One way or another, we must explore the kinds of institutions that go beyond the conventional models to deal with the real facts about the activities that bear on the welfare of the people.

My modest ambition is merely to expose the need for such new thinking about the institutions of representative government, not to prescribe a method for reform or sketch particular reforms. It will take far more work to compile all the laws, rules, and practices that in fact govern the crucial processes of linking and decision making that I point to and to find the ways to reform those institutions to improve the performance of representative democracy.

The six sets of facts and the false assumptions about their relationship to democratic institutions are briefly recapitulated:

• The first problematic assumption is that representative democracy is only about linking a fixed set of people, the citizens, to decision makers so that their interests are promoted and the decision makers are held accountable. The fact is that to promote the interests of the core citizenry, however defined, representative institutions have to link the decision-making process to many noncitizens present in the territory (chapter 3). Just as with the core citizens, decision makers must be aware of the preferences of the these quasi-citizens and secure their cooperation with and compliance to laws and policies. The implication is not only that these resident quasi-citizens have to be represented in the system, but that, since they are a set of people that changes from time to time and from issue to issue, the links that convey their preferences and secure their cooperation are specialized and constantly adapting as well.

• The second problematic assumption is that political decision making relevant to representative democracy is about making laws and policies to be applied within the territorial jurisdiction over which the political system is sovereign. It is believed that action in other jurisdictions is a form of "foreign policy" whose representativeness is secured primarily by holding chief executives accountable. The fact is that all political actors at many levels are heavily involved in making policies that are meant to have influence in other jurisdictions—not only in other countries, but also in supranational entities (such as international organizations) and subnational entities (such as states and provinces in federal systems as well as indigenous enclaves) (chapter 4). The implication is that to promote the interests of the core citizenry, decision makers must link to both the government and the population in another jurisdiction that are stakeholders for a particular issue. Knowing what works requires not just diplomatic contact and expert knowledge, but ongoing interactive contact like that which decision makers have with the core citizens. The reality of rapidly changing situations in the other jurisdictions reemphasizes the need for constantly changing decision networks.

• The third problematic assumption is that the set of interests of the people is relatively stable and that organizational dimensions of their links to the political system, principally political parties and civil society associations, are stable, too. Thus, the assumption goes, the main challenge of building a representative government—for example, securing greater equality—is to incorporate into the decision-making process organizations that represent less-favored people. The fact is that the sets of interests of the people are too complex to be simply matched with the goals of civil society associations and that the organizations change rapidly (chapter 6). Political parties and long-lasting interest or advocacy groups become broad umbrellas, linking multiple and changing sets of interests. Most civil society associations, in their role as policy advocates, either dissolve or form ever-shifting alliances to accomplish their objectives. The rise of digital communication makes it possible for new sets of groups to form and adapt rapidly to changing patterns of interests, although it is certainly not inevitable, and slow, faulty, or manipulated adaptation may lead to injustice. Norms, practices, and laws shape the patterns and could be reformed.

• The fourth problematic assumption is that the presence of personal ties in modern politics beyond the family sphere (where they remain expected) is a sign of domination of some leaders over their followers or of corruption and favoritism. Older theories of "modernization" predicted that these particularistic relations, considered private and irrelevant to "real" politics, would fade as universalistic ones became dominant. The fact is that personal networks are a crucial and often positive component of the links between the people and the decision makers, particularly when decision networks are adapting (or not) to rapidly changing conditions (chapter 7).

• The fifth problematic assumption is that political decision making is summed up as a process in which actors with given sets of interests either interact strategically to arrive at a distribution of available goods among them or confront one another with competing moral principles. The system is democratic, according to this conception, if all the relevant interests are represented in the process, the competition takes place on a "level playing field," the bargains are fair, and the moral differences are respected. But facts, explanations, and interpretations are introduced into the process and affect the rationality of actors' strategies, the viability of bargains, and the relevance of moral concessions. The fact is that this information is transformed in the course of political decision making. The quality of the deliberation that evaluates and transforms it has a major impact on the effectiveness and justice of outcomes (chapter 9). Further, new information that emerges from research or deliberation may well change the nature of the moral problem, the identity of the interests, and the opportunities for individual and collective success. Information not only is utilized by actors promoting their own interests, but is processed interactively, and what was a common understanding at the beginning of the decision-making process may be fundamentally altered.

• The sixth problematic assumption is that the decision making whose reform would significantly improve democracy is that which takes place at the end stages of the lawmaking process. It is believed that while the many demands, elements of information, and moral positions go through diverse channels, what counts for results—and, therefore, for whether the system is democratic—is the last stage, symbolized by the legislators writing and adopting laws and the executive signing and promulgating them. The fact is that the work of bargaining, moral argument, and deliberation—that is, the substance of decision making on which serving the public interest depends—is carried out in many venues in the polity (chapter 10). For some of these, including subordinate or superior units in a federation and autonomous agencies, the relation to the main decision-making processes is regulated and ordered for effectiveness and justice (with varying success). But a very significant number of pathways for "almost final" decision making, which I call "decision networks," have less formal guidelines and highly erratic informal regulations, despite their importance.

No one seriously believes these false assumptions anymore: that the political system can escape external forces or that all crucial decisions are made on the floor of legislatures. No one believes that given sets of interests are permanently the dominant players in the system. No one seriously believes that politics is just a strategic game to determine who gets what and not a process to solve problems. At least no one would act on those assumptions. Yet they are commonplaces of conventional analysis. From the standpoint of social science, they have become obstacles to effective democratic reform. From the standpoint of taking action, an argument can be made for ignoring details to get things done. But it is always dangerous, and when the "details" are as important as each of the six facts, simplifications become destructive. A new agenda of reform is necessary.

NOTES ON THE AGENDA FOR REFORM

It should be emphasized that even though the facts point to situations not usually understood to be part of political institutions, they are governed by enforceable norms and standards of procedure—both formal and informal—and are thus institutionalized. I say "are" and not "should be" because, except in moments of confusion or dissolution, there are laws, norms, and practices that influence and shape these activities of the political system.

We are not used to thinking of the jumble of special working groups that advise a president, the friendship-based links of politicians and political activists, or the links of a military commander with the leaders of the communities that his troops are occupying as being institutionalized and rule based. And they would not be if we thought of institutions only in legal terms. But there are enforceable norms involved in all these cases. The president is under pressure to include a wide range of opinions, knowledgeable people, and diverse stakeholders in a working group that he or she establishes. These norms may be enforced by the participants, the media, or even the president's spouse. Investigative reporters and rivals may call attention to biases and "inappropriate" relations between politicians and advocates. The military commander may be given very specific instructions from his superiors about his relationships with village leaders. Not all these sets of norms will be designed to produce benefits for the core citizens—that is, be democratic. But they are norms and, as such, can be reformed for various purposes, including democracy.

In each case, these are a jumble of emergent norms, consciously adopted rules for other purposes, outdated laws, and inappropriate old ideas. Improving democratic performance requires rethinking the practices and rules in order to change them to accomplish the goals of a democracy, to promote law and policy in the interest of the people.

Institutional reform takes many forms. It may involve rewriting constitutions or the formal laws that govern the process of representation. But it also may consist of drawing up guidelines to bring informal practices into alignment with the law or one another, prominent leaders setting exemplary models, or formalizing norms that emerge from the interaction of many who are involved and wish to see something positive come from their activity. If I am right that these areas of political action are important for realizing democracy and that there is a need for reform, then the job is to discover what new norms and new ways of encouraging better performance are necessary.

A different sort of question about the implication for democracy of these facts is to suggest other goals for reformers than to make the output of the system provide benefits for the people. Some would say that we are suggesting that institutions be built to control activity that should be left to the people. If by that is meant that micro-managing people can have negative consequences, it is true. If it means that we should never seek to find a way to set standards, issue guidelines, make people aware of the consequences of their actions, and try to improve them, then it is false. If it means that the dangers of threats to the rights and freedoms of the citizens and of oppression by potential dictators or of special interests are more important than the dangers of inequality, reckless executives, corruption, and potential stalemate in the face of recession, climate change, and ecological threats, then I believe that this is a discussion that should be opened.

The areas of needed reforms suggested by the six facts can be thought of as falling into three broad areas that, I believe, sum up the main tasks of a new agenda for the reform of democracies. Each them involves conceptualizing democratic politics in a way that differs from the conventions that form the basis of the models of representative democracy outlined in chapter 1. They concern the formation and operation of decision networks, which suggests that democratic politics is about flexible problem solving; the establishment of standards for handling information, which looks at democratic politics as thoughtful collective action; and the inclusion of quasi-citizen stakeholders, which implies breaking free of the nation-state limits that have shaped our view of democracy.

Other foci could be drawn from the six facts. Reforms of the classic institutions will continue to be necessary. Dealing with the problems of inequality, corruption, executive recklessness, and inability to deal with crises will require many reforms as well, probably as many policies and social-movement confrontations. But these three areas are essential targets of any serious reform, whatever else is needed. The task of democratic reformers will be to discover specific ways to reach these targets. Here are some notes on what might be reformed in each of these three areas.

DEMOCRATIC POLITICS AS FLEXIBLE PROBLEM SOLVING

Again and again in this book, I have suggested that for a representative democracy to be successful in serving its core citizenry, it has to build and rebuild decision networks to handle new information, include new stakeholders, and/or tackle new problems, and then redirect or dismantle them when events and issues change again.

This continual reconfiguration has always taken place, and the classic institutions of democracy were intended to provide a framework for it. But the dynamics that we thought could be contained in a democratic fashion by elections, legislatures, party systems, and even pluralist interest groups are taking a new shape in the era of the Internet, global connections, and the growing number of highly specialized people. Creating a stable regime of any kind requires the formulation of some general principles, norms, or laws that will allow the dynamic process to happen productively. One way to interpret the message of this book is that the old stabilizing frames are no longer sufficient and thus new ones are needed. It is worth emphasizing that this dynamism is at the heart of politics. The goal of reforming the institutions of democracy—despite the emphasis on stability that the word "institution" implies—is to make this continual change more vibrant and successful in solving new problems and guiding collective action in the interests of the people.

To suggest how to think of institutions that shape the process of changing decision networks, we might note a parallel. As a set of people with links to society and called together to propose ways to confront problems, based on their understanding of the possible causes, decision networks have much in common with legislatures.

The legislature itself can, indeed, be thought of as a type of decision network. Pre-democratic models were a form of working group established by a monarch to link him to his principal sources of support, financial and military. They became the central democratic institution after they won their right to have their proposals heard and then obeyed by the monarch, built methods of deliberation, and, crucially, established a way of being linked to the people, first by means of elections and then through political parties.

Decision networks and legislatures have similar pathologies (from the point of view of democracy), and therefore should get the attention of the institution builder (and reformer). Historically, legislatures had to fight to have their proposals considered as authoritative. Constitutions were written to spell out just what their authority was. The constructed decision networks to confront problems now have no such constitutionally defined access to authoritative power centers, but they are able to take advantage of special relationships with the legislators or executives who set them up. Reformers should consider the ways in which decisions become authoritative.

In both legislatures and decision networks, representation may be skewed, favoring links with one set of stakeholders over others. A legislature may not have members from a minority ethnic group or even anyone who can speak for it. A working group established to consider policy with regard to bank failures may not have members with the kinds of links with everyday depositors to represent that interest in the decision-making process.

Decision networks created ad hoc to deal with particular problems presumably have the freedom—if they have the will—to tailor their membership, and thus their links, to the needs and demands of the problems. Legislatures, usually thought to be representative of the "whole society" (presumably, the core citizenry), must find a general rule that specifies how the members are allocated, by territorial divisions in many cases. This may produce a just distribution among those needing representation (certainly, the intention of early reformers) or, being nonspecific and relatively fixed, may not embrace the people relevant to many of the issues that arise. For example, legislatures have not always represented all races in society, and, in the current globalizing world, they are in a poor position to represent quasi-citizens. The norms used to select participants of working groups are a major point of investigation—and reform.

Another broad criterion for a successful legislature or decision network is the existence of a method to seek out the facts and theories and integrate them into a decision-making process that allows for genuine deliberation. Legislatures have developed all sorts of ways to do this: committees, hearings, closed and open meetings, and special offices and staffs. If the current experience with economic crises in the United States and Europe is any sign, however, the chances of real deliberation taking place in legislatures are modest. The ad hoc working group may be structured specifically around the fact-finding and deliberation process (and may be the means through which some legislatures carry out deliberation), but being ad hoc, it may be too specific and require fundamental change (perhaps even termination and reconstitution) to achieve anything like an adequate information-gathering and deliberative process when the issue it was created to consider evolves.

The ability of legislatures to react to a crisis is constantly being tested and depends a great deal on leadership and flexibility. Presumably, decision networks have the advantage of being formed in order to deal with specific problems and ought to be in a good position to respond, but that depends on the method of establishing them. When it is an act of an executive authority, a network's effectiveness depends on the capacity of that authority to identify the problem and choose the participants. If a decision network emerges from the people who are being affected by the crisis, the context will matter. Traditions of confrontation (from whatever side) may push the network into conflict rather than problem-solving mode. If it is a highly technical problem, such a health issue, the network may be skewed in favor of the people who know the issue—doctors and representatives of pharmaceutical companies, presumably. If new technology changes the issue, they will understand what is changing, although that is no guarantee that they will adapt effectively.

Because decision networks are set up for a specific purpose, some of their particular qualities demand attention. The danger of undermining the search for information and serious deliberation may come from criteria for membership in the group, which could include prior agreement among the appointees about a particular solution to the problem they are supposed to be considering. That is what is alleged, at least, for the network established to decide whether to invade Iraq and Afghanistan in order to deal with terrorism. It is also a frequent charge when a working group is formed by a partisan organization. A labor-based, left-oriented city administration may appoint a group to propose an educational policy. It may be that the members were chosen because they had reaffirmed their commitment to traditional-style labor unions, which may rule out certain options. Making sure the members come to the group without preconceptions would be one of the considerations for a reformer.

A particular problem of decision networks is that their effectiveness is usually time delimited, and the norms governing them should include a sunset clause or an agreement about the circumstances under which they are to be dismantled or reconstructed. As ad hoc groups, when conditions change, their purpose either changes or disappears. The dangers to effectiveness or skewed representation may come from old networks trying to perform new tasks.

The role of personal relationships in forming working groups may be crucial. Individual networking in the fields of law- and policy making may be important to choosing the members of decision networks. Since they often are established to deal with new problems, there is little in the way of standard norms for guiding recruitment. "Merit-based" recruitment presumes that specific, known skills and knowledge can be the basis for recruitment, but the relevant skills and knowledge may be a concern that the group has to discuss. Personal networking is often a better means to explore who is thinking about an issue. The digital connections promoted in social-networking sites often are touted as a way to make friends, but they can identify needed skills and common concerns as well. Although social-networking sites may not shape major decision networks now, their growth and diversification suggest that they may play a role in the future.

Other issues may be brought up about these groups by comparing them with legislatures. For example, they lack the formalized system of accountability through elections, but dismissal by the authority that appointed them is a much more flexible tool than periodic elections. Making that tool serve the public interest is obviously a challenge. The same is true of elections. Elections are too often very expensive and crude instruments for achieving accountability. Transparency of operation is another consideration, since very often these groups are set up to work behind the scenes, sometimes for good reasons. Reformers have a lot of work to do.

DEMOCRATIC POLITICS AS THOUGHTFUL
COLLECTIVE ACTION

The second dimension of the interactions between the decision makers and the people that has to be thought through to reform the institutions of representative democracy concerns information and deliberation. Attention to these aspects of decision making means thinking of politics as making possible rational collective action in the interests of the people. It differs from the common emphasis on considering the essence of politics as reconciling conflicts and finding the basis for living together. The objectives are not incompatible, but different. If the focus is on how the political system can act, and act for the people, then attention to the way it processes information in deciding laws and policies is crucial.

Misinformation about the capacities of women, the results of the use of overwhelming force in Iraq, the political impact of bank or country bailouts, and the efficacy of dealing with addiction by outlawing the possession and dealing of drugs, among other topics, has caused significant damage to the people's welfare. Making laws and adopting policies that are good for the people depend on the quality of the information on which the laws and policies are based. But that quality is not the product of an information bank run by a library, university researchers, or a Web site. Good information no doubt builds on sources like these. But especially for policy, it is the way in which such information is brought into the decision-making process, evaluated, transformed, and applied that counts.

One might assume that good information and deliberation would be a concern only when thinking about the effectiveness of policy decisions, not their democratic quality. But since I am using the criterion of output for the people as the measure of democracy, it matters to democratic reforms. Getting the problem and its solution right is crucial to maximizing public welfare. Deliberation involves an ongoing process of defining and redefining the problems, conditions, goals, and stakeholders. Information is not a neutral set of facts and theories that experts know and can put to the service of any goal that they are given. Information interacts with the situation and emerges out of practice.

The demands for information change rapidly. A question about the status of a set of firms and their workers may turn rapidly into a question about the clash of cultures, with migrants who work in those companies being rejected by natives, along with a concern about regional security. The demands for information may be about new interests (such as the impact of foreign imports on the markets that domestic firms have had to themselves) and new kinds of problems (such as the impact of the costs of new technology on domestic firms). A set of democratic institutions must keep up with those changes, with the input of people knowledgeable in the new configurations, so that the outcomes of decisions will serve the various people who are affected by them. It is almost inevitable that there will have to be new "experts" and/or that the experts will need very complex linkages to old and new groups.

Generating data, explanatory theories, and relevant interpretations in this rapidly changing environment is a challenge, but it is one that many organizations and even individuals constantly confront. A flexible working group obviously has this potential, bringing together researchers and practitioners and experienced administrators.

Imagine a policy discussion about encouraging investment in distribution outlets by a foreigner whose company produces a good in his home country. The decision makers must know facts about the stability or growth potential of the manufacturer and its history with child labor or exploitation. They have to have convincing theories about the factors propelling the foreign producer and the impact of the investment on local industries. The decision makers also want to hear the interpretations about the significance of foreign presence in the industry, given worldwide trends. The deliberation would not get far or would move in false directions without information like this. No matter whether the decision makers want to weigh the interests of the core citizenry much higher than those of the foreign investor or not, whether they regard the foreign businessman as a potential core citizen or a potential exploiter, they still need that information. In our interpenetrated world, good information about others is more and more crucial.

But, of course, gathering information is not the most difficult problem. With the digital revolution and the spread of education, the world is characterized by a plethora of information, not a dearth of it. With the flood of information available on the Internet, it is important not only to introduce information, but especially to evaluate it and integrate it with other information.

What should we watch for as legislatures, executives, political parties, and decision networks process information? Much attention has been paid to this deliberative aspect of politics in the past few decades, especially under the impulse given by Jürgen Habermas, building on his theory of communication.[2] Scholars and observers have gone in several directions with his ideas.

Some have tried to formulate ideal forms of deliberation.[3] Much writing about deliberation falls under the rubric of "deliberative democracy." It has asked a different question from the one posed here: How to bring more of the people into the discussion, how to democratize the debate by incorporating more people into it.[4] Schemes ranging from periodic public discussions to wide-open debates online have been explored.[5] Sometimes it is assumed that incorporating more people into the discussion will increase the benefits to the people, but that is not necessarily so.[6] Another goal perhaps achieved by popular inclusion is to focus not so much on the effectiveness or justice of the decisions, but on their legitimacy.[7] Here, "deliberation" will mean assessing the validity of information and applying it to the law or policy.

Norms for assessing information abound. Many scholarly fields as well as organizations have complex rules and understandings about what information counts. Scientists have norms about evidence and causal inference, including peer review and replication. Academics have procedures for citation and review. Journalists have rules about what corroboration ought to be available before publishing, and professional associations have guidelines about who has the competence to judge. Transferring any one of these standards to the political world without modification is probably inappropriate.[8] But some principles are imperative. A politician who cites a public-opinion poll as proof of the desirability of a program he favors should be subject to demands for confirmation, not only of the data themselves, but of their relevance. The endless claims that doing one thing or another will bring on or avert a military, an economic, or a climate "crisis"; that promoting unionization in public education will hurt or help students; that lowering taxes will raise or lower economic activity –all should automatically require a reality test and public acknowledgment of that need. The assertion about the presence of weapons of mass destruction in Iraq before the invasion by the United States, for example, should have been subject to a much more rigorous evaluation by academics, policy analysts, diplomats, and intelligence operatives than it was.

The argument that information, opinions, claims, and even prejudices and proposals grounded purely on imagined facts have a claim to being protected is based on the supposition that encouraging a wide range of ideas will more likely lead to the truth than would restricting "false" ones. On this or similar bases, a plausible argument for democratic norms covering information is that nothing should be prohibited. But freedom of expression does not extend to what happens after information has been introduced. The competition among ideas that is so prized should be turned into a dialectical process, not just a confrontation. Deliberation is dynamic. People with one view listen and learn from others with competing ones. The most important test of information, especially in decision making, is whether it can stand up to criticism coming from a different angle. The outcome, in well-conducted deliberation, is not a compromise on which set of facts or theories is true, but a synthesis of both. In this world saturated with the half-truths of advertising, such deliberation is essential.

Not only the validation of the accuracy of information, but the process of bringing evidence to bear on questions of law and policy require attention. In the current efforts in the United States to deal with the world economic crisis, there is a lot of information about the economic conditions themselves as well as many theories about the causes and their impacts— for example, bank strategies on risky loans, China's aggressive policies on trade, the difficulties faced by major economic sectors like the automobile industry, the creation of such fictive resources as derivatives, and the weakness of American education in math and science. The methods the polity has for dealing with all the facts and all the theories range widely, from setting up special commissions, to encouraging public discussions by and among economists and policy makers, to media presentations of the opinions of "people on the street" who presumably are being affected by the economic recession.

At many points, reasonable norms are invoked, and a well-grounded policy emerges. But the process is fraught with miscellaneous "noise," including statements of moral principles announced as fact: government intervention, being evil, is counterproductive; the banks are exploiters of the people, so punishing them will help the economy. Reconciling divergent goals is complicated enough without a norm of political debate that does not value serious deliberation.

The task of identifying the reforms that would increase the quality of information that both enters and emerges from a deliberative process is enormous. It is asking for institutions not simply to guide a particular debate about policy or law, but to shape the search for information about an ever-changing set of issues. It is a task whose success is necessary for reform.

DEMOCRACY NOT BOUND TO THE NATION-STATE

The third area of political action beyond the usual understanding of the institutions of representative democracy that needs reform concerns the group of people I have called "quasi-citizens," those who have an important stake in the decisions being made but who are not members of the group chosen to be the core citizenry. The multiplicity and importance of quasi-citizens suggest that we must loosen the hold of the idea that democratic politics is something that the people do within the jurisdictional boundaries of a nation-state and is built on those who constitute a nation. The assumption is understandable because regimes that are considered democratic were developed in a historical period when the nation state was becoming the dominant form of the polity and all emphasis was on the relationships within that nation and state. The current trend toward "globalization" weakens the dominance of the nation-state in many ways, and the facts about quasi-citizens constitute one aspect of that change. The boundaries of the contemporary state remain important for specifying the extent of legal jurisdiction, among other reasons. But the practical consequence of the continued interpenetration and interdependence of countries is that political regimes are no longer confined by territorial boundaries. The presence of many non-nationals within a territory makes the idea of "nation" problematic, and the importance of people in jurisdictions other than the nation for making laws and policies renders the significance of boundaries problematic. Many have noted the global reach of major governments and the interdependence of economic and cultural forces, but it is less usual to draw conclusions about representation and representative democracy from that reach and interdependence. However the core citizenry is defined, the representative process will be structured to reach the quasi-citizens, which will result in a system much less self-contained then the conventional notion of a polity, democratic or not. Democratic reforms must pay attention to how quasi-citizens are linked to decision makers because these links will affect whether the system acts in the interests of the core citizenry. The channels of communication include the domestic and foreign intelligence agencies of the government, scholarly research, the public and specialized media, the new connections on the Web, clashes on the street between quasi-citizens and law-enforcement officers, diplomatic correspondence, and personal connections of travelers, investors, and technicians who work with the quasi-citizens.

Reforms intended to promote democratic outcomes of law- and policy making will have to ensure that quasi-citizens are linked to decision makers in a fashion that is similar in many respects to the way in which core citizens are. The goal is to make sure that decisions are received by the quasi-citizens with compliance and cooperation, that they will not be resisted effectively. Domination and even physical force might accomplish that goal, although even these sorts of links would have to be based on an understanding of what the quasi-citizens want and are likely to do in response. And to know that, the decision makers must have the two-way information flow that they have with the core citizens. And that means that quasi-citizens have to have the same, as well as some form of accountability mechanism.

The most obvious difference between quasi- and core citizens in terms of their communication with decision makers is, of course, that only core citizens vote in elections (assuming that core citizens are the same as legal citizens). Election campaigns do not leave quasi-citizens out of the two-way communication—especially those within a country who observe them—although as members of groups not being directly courted by candidates, the political messages may not be as effective with quasi-citizens as they are with core citizens. Some quasi-citizens may, of course, be in a position to finance candidates or issue ultimatums (say, NATO on the occasion of elections in the Middle East), which may have a significant effect on the outcome of an election. But from the standpoint of institutions, the disenfranchisement of quasi-citizens means that they do not share with core citizens the accountability device that most think of as the ultimate tool against straying leaders.

But however crucial elections are, they are a very blunt instrument for anyone to use in order to influence policy. Although the language surrounding them appears to focus heavily on policy, in fact the increasingly permanent campaigns are a (very expensive) way to select leaders, to the point that many people now use the word "politics" to refer to the process of winning elections, rather than making collective decisions. And there are many other accountability mechanisms. Quasi-citizens must have the capacity to reward and punish decision makers—in other words, to hold them accountable in some degree for their decisions—even if it is only in withholding the cooperation necessary for the success of a policy.

Most of the real work of representation is done not through elections, but through many other channels. Although the difference between an immigrant working for citizenship in the United States and an Afghan villager under American occupation—both quasi-citizens—is enormous, quasi-citizens on the whole are more likely than core citizens to be distanced, speak different languages, be shielded or supported by other governments, or be required to limit or make secret their political involvement. And although the involvement of core citizens in the political process may in fact be erratic, quasi-citizens are more likely to be involved more episodically, being very issue dependent. But on the whole, the problems of establishing the links between quasi-citizens and decision makers are very much like those with core citizens.

The challenge is to make sure that information is accurate, that it is fed into the decision-making process suitably, and that it is processed and discussed in such a way as to verify and apply the knowledge effectively. These are the same concerns as those for improving the representation of core citizens, and they also are subject to the problems associated with the multiplicity and changing alliances of decision networks. The unusual demand is that these concerns be applied to quasi-citizens.

This is not an argument that quasi-citizens be favored less or more than they are, only that their reactions to laws and policies have an important effect on the welfare of the core citizens, and therefore democratic reform must be concerned with them.

There are moral and practical issues, of course, about the balance of benefits. If gains for the quasi-citizens mean that the core citizens will lose—that is, if it is a zero-sum situation—then only the core citizens win in a democratic system. When a set of people decide that they can benefit only by injuring others, democracy might sanction it. This is not a question about democracy, but about the way people treat one another.

Although there is too much violence between people in the world today, in many cases the outlook is much more positive; what benefits the core citizens very often requires the compliance and cooperation of quasi-citizens, and that offers some benefits to the quasi-citizens. The difference in outcomes for the two sets of citizens is often not as great as it may seem.

A related moral question concerns the political decision that determines just who are the core citizens and, therefore, where the line is drawn between core and quasi-citizens. It is a political choice, since "core citizenry" is not a category that derives from the actual workings of the policy-making process (as is "stakeholder"). Rather, it is made by the people in power. This decision is made concrete in the formal requirements established for citizenship, but there is always considerable disagreement and fuzziness about who should be considered one of "us" and who is one of "them." That decision identifies the "people" whose interests are promoted by a democratic regime. Thus it is a crucial decision that conditions what reforms are needed. If the definition of core citizens is narrow—say, embracing only the dominant ethnic group—democratic reforms would be different than if the category included broadly everyone who lives within the territory of a nation-state or anyone who accepts the authority of the political system. An odd result is that the decision about who the people are who benefit from democracy is not likely to be a democratic decision. Only if it was accepted that all stakeholders are the "people"—in other words, leaving out the category of quasi-citizen entirely—would the identification of the "people" be considered not a political decision, determined by relative power.

A possible but highly optimistic vision of the future is that the gap between core and quasi-citizens may shrink and that decision makers will not only take all stakeholders into account, but give them equal weight in determining the outcomes of law- and policy making. Then politics would really be about problem solving and not division of the spoils.[9] But for the time being, it is necessary to keep the two apart in our analysis. The representation of quasi-citizens remains a crucial step.

The reform of institutions with the intent to improve democratic performance has to confront the fact that much of the political action is taking place outside the conventional institutions of representative democratic governance, which have been with us for centuries. We have to turn our attention to these sorts of activities and devise reforms for the institutions that currently shape them. Shaping the way in which decision networks are built and dismantled, information is processed in decision making, and noncitizen stakeholders are brought into the system is challenging in part because we are not used to thinking of decision networks, information, and quasi-citizens in our conventional views of political institutions. I suggest that institutionalization and institutional reform are both possible and necessary. They are possible because these practices are in fact governed by norms and rules, and the challenge is to change the rules, not create them. They are necessary because unless we find other means, not reforming political institutions is to accept the level of inequality, the reckless leaders, the corruption, and the stalemates that are endemic to the system. But I believe that is unacceptable and that the reform of political institutions to achieve a better democracy is mandatory. For that, it will be necessary to broaden our notions of these institutions and the political action they regulate.

There is much to do.

Notes

INTRODUCTION

1. The obvious reference is to Marx's understanding of Hegelian dialectics, but it has become a widespread line of thinking, perhaps to avoid the hard work of finding out what might work—or at least putting it off until after the revolution.

2. C. Tilly and S. G. Tarrow, *Contentious Politics* (Boulder, Colo.: Paradigm, 2007).

3. Particularly in *On Liberty*. See J. S. Mill, *On Liberty and Other Essays*, ed. J. Gray (Oxford: Oxford University Press, 2008).

4. A. de Tocqueville, *Democracy in America and Two Essays on America*, trans. G. E. Bevan, ed. I. Kramnick (1835; London: Penguin, 2003).

5. R. D. Putnam, R. Leonardi, and R. Y. Nanetti, *Making Democracy Work: Civic Traditions in Modern Italy* (Princeton, N.J.: Princeton University Press, 1994); and many others.

6. I tried my hand at answering these questions in D. A. Chalmers, "What Is It About Associations in Civil Society That Promotes Democracy?" (http://www.columbia.edu/~chalmers/AssocDem.html).

7. The classic argument is made by Mill in *On Liberty*, but even his "harm principle"—that one should be allowed to say anything that does not

cause harm to others—is not very clear about how remote that "harm" might be.

8. On Brazil, see, for example, L. E. Armijo, P. Faucher, and M. Dembinska, "Compared to What? Assessing Brazil's Political Institutions," *Comparative Political Studies* 39, no. 6 (2006): 759–786. China, with its history of explicitly anti-Western notions of democracy, will present a greater challenge to judgments, assuming that its leaders do not suddenly change course and adopt a two-party system.

I. RETHINKING THE INSTITUTIONS OF REPRESENTATIVE DEMOCRACY

1. This formulation leaves many terms unspecified. Who are "the people"? Although I will deal with this question in part II, it is fundamentally ambiguous and relying on conventional wisdom might be dangerous, but I think that it is understandable and meaningful. And what are "the people's interests"? Again, I believe that the phrase is intuitively plausible and at least as likely to be precise as the "rule of law" and "defense of rights" or "accountability." In this book, I do not need a precise measurement of democracy, only a way of thinking about it.

2. The polis in Aristotle's *Politics* presented an ideal of all citizens sharing in decision making, but of course the citizens were a small part of the population, and the polis was small. Even then, Aristotle, and many others after, felt that a mixed regime was the best system of governance. The ideal, however, has been held out for millennia. In *The Social Contract*, which established the important principle of popular sovereignty, Rousseau implied that all citizens would participate in decision making, but he was notoriously vague about how that would happen and is usually taken as having favored small polities.

3. There are many studies of the successes and weakness of such efforts. Recently, the concern with "deliberative democracy" has focused attention on mechanisms for encouraging not just the making of decisions by the people who are affected by them, but also the deliberations about the policies. For more on this, see chapter 9.

4. My definition is related to the distinction between "output" and "input" democracy. See R. Bellamy, "Democracy Without Democracy? Can the EU's Democratic 'Outputs' Be Separated from the Democratic 'Inputs'

Provided by Competitive Parties and Majority Rule?" *Journal of European Public Policy* 17, no. 1 (2010): 2–19. I shall use a much broader concept of "inputs."

5. H. F. Pitkin, *The Concept of Representation* (Berkeley: University of California Press, 1967); J. Mansbridge, "Rethinking Representation," *American Political Science Review* 97, no. 4 (2003): 515–528. But L. Disch argues that even Pitkin, in her classic work, showed signs of recognizing the limitations of this conception of representation, in "Rethinking Responsiveness," Western Political Science Association 2010 Annual Meeting Paper, Social Science Research Network, http://ssrn.com/abstract=1580937.

6. In the revolutions of the seventeenth and eighteenth centuries, beginning with the Glorious Revolution of 1688, parliaments were considered the main challengers to royal absolutist authority and became the main link between the decision makers and the people who counted. These assemblies consisted of members who were chosen by influential citizens in particular districts throughout the country and who represented them. Other groups and individuals came to replace the earlier landowners, church leaders, and local notables in selecting the deputies. But assemblies of representatives of geographic or social units remained a key link between the people and the decision makers.

7. One sample of work that undercuts the centrality of the single representative includes E. Peruzzotti, "Constituents, Representatives and the Dual Politics of Democratic Representation," 2009, Social Science Research Network, http://ssrn.com/abstract=1653510. Another includes R. E. Goodin, who examines the possibilities of representatives being "like" those they represent and opts for a logic that presents the "fact of diversity," not literal re-presenting, in "Representing Diversity," *British Journal of Political Science* 34, no. 3 (2004): 453–468.

8. A cynical view that too easily arises from this conception of representation is that all these other actors in the system are not elected representatives, so they must be representatives nonetheless because they are "bought and paid for" by someone.

9. I am aware that I am avoiding the question of whether there are anything like "real" interests of the people as a whole. Despite the popularity of a constructivist point of view, according to which something like the interests of the people is just what they agree it is, I am proceeding on the notion that there is a standard used to judge popular opinion. At the least, there is

good reason to believe that there is always a basis for critique of any particular momentary belief by more serious consideration. Thus there is always a "more true" set of people's interest, which is sufficient here.

10. Aristotle's notion of the "polity" as composed of democratic and aristocratic elements is about the best description of a practical-ideal regime. He always assumes that the interest of the group—the community, the polity members—is paramount. The "polity" is not an "-ocracy" because neither the demos nor the aristocrats "rule" (which implies rule over). The trouble is that "polity" has come to be devoid of any normative content. One can say "more democratic" or "more aristocratic," but not more "polity-ic." The word "representative" is attractive because it is both a noun and a normative adjective. It also serves to point to the interactive component of government. But it is very hard to use "representative" without talking about "re-presenting" the pieces, a temptation to be resisted.

11. There are many descriptions of this process, from H. D. Lasswell, *Politics: Who Gets What, When, How. With Postscript (1958)* (1936; New York: Meridian Books, 1958), to J. W. Kingdon, *Agendas, Alternatives, and Public Policies* (New York: Longman, 2003), to others. I do not claim any special utility for my brief outline.

12. For a review and perceptive disaggregation of the elements, see J. L. Cohen, "Changing Paradigms of Citizenship and the Exclusiveness of the Demos," *International Sociology* 14, no. 3 (1999): 245–268. See also E. F. Cohen, *Semi-Citizenship in Democratic Politics* (New York: Cambridge University Press, 2009).

13. That no leader, for more than a moment, can know the interests of the people without intense links is an assertion of fact. It is crucial to my argument. I do not believe that anyone would seriously challenge its validity, although that nature of those links is very much an open question.

14. Disch offers an interesting analysis about the interactive quality in "Rethinking Responsiveness." The philosophical discussion about the meaning and reality of the interaction for democratic theory is very extensive. An excellent summary is in N. Urbinati and M. E. Warren, "The Concept of Representation in Contemporary Democratic Theory," *Annual Review of Political Science* 11 (2008): 387–412.

15. During the process, good institutions might help control many kinds of problems: misperception, willful favoritism, and debilitating conflict or stalemating polarization. At this point, however, I do not want to

address the problem of what the institutions should do, merely where they should be.

16. On a similar, but more extreme, note, Rousseau's grant of absolute authority to the "General Will" makes sense only as what the people would want if they had complete information and infinite time to discuss it.

17. P. C. Schmitter and T. L. Karl, "What Democracy Is . . . and Is Not," *Journal of Democracy* 2, no. 4 (1991): 75–88.

18. The minimalist Schumpeterian view that equates democracy with effective elections relies exclusively on this accountability mechanism to intimidate lawmakers into representing the people. See J. A. Schumpeter, *Capitalism, Socialism, and Democracy* (New York: Harper & Row, 1975).

19. J. Locke, *Second Treatise of Government*, ed. C. B. Macpherson (1690; Indianapolis: Hackett, 1980).

20. Since the models are additive for the most part, whatever clarity they have is in theoretical terms, as in Weber's famous "ideal types." See M. Weber, *The Methodology of the Social Sciences*, ed. and trans. E. A. Shils and H. A. Finch (1903–1917; New York: Free Press, 1997).

21. The classic statement of this form is E. Burke, *Reflections on the Revolution in France* (1790; Oxford: Oxford University Press, 2009). Burke placed greater emphasis on knowledge of the world and less on knowledge of the people living in the territory the deputies were nominally representing.

22. P. C. Schmitter and G. Lehmbruch, *Trends Toward Corporatist Intermediation* (Beverly Hills, Calif.: Sage, 1979).

23. C. Tilly and S. G. Tarrow, *Contentious Politics* (Boulder, Colo.: Paradigm, 2007). An interesting effort to specify the criteria for success in a contentious polity can be found in Sidney Tarrow's interesting discussion of the conditions for successful change for social movements ranging from student demonstrations in France in the 1960s to the women's movement in the United States. See S. G. Tarrow, *Power in Movement: Social Movements and Contentious Politics* (Cambridge: Cambridge University Press, 1998).

2. WHICH "PEOPLE" ARE REPRESENTED IN A REPRESENTATIVE DEMOCRACY?

1. The classic statement of this is E. J. Sieyès, *What Is the Third Estate?* (New York: Praeger, 1964).

2. See the discussion in B. R. O. G. Anderson, *Imagined Communities: Reflections on the Origin and Spread of Nationalism* (London: Verso, 2006).

3. Despite the importance of the decision about who the core citizenry is to be, in this book I do not talk about how it is made, since it is assumed rather than problematized in my definition of "democracy."

4. R. Bauböck develops the "stakeholder" principle in "Stakeholder Citizenship and Transnational Political Participation: A Normative Evaluation of External Voting," *Fordham Law Review* 75, no. 5 (2007): 2393–2447, and "Global Justice, Freedom of Movement and Democratic Citizenship," *European Journal of Sociology / Archives européennes de sociologie* 50, no. 1 (2009): 1–31. These two articles are relevant particularly to the discussions of "quasi-citizens" in chapters 3 and 4. Bauböck is more concerned with citizenship than representation. He says at one point, "Everyone who is affected by a decision has a claim that her interests should be taken into account but not everyone has a claim to be a member of the political community on whose behalf the decision is taken" ("Global Justice," 21).

5. A further complicating factor is that the welfare of the core citizens may depend on the welfare of the quasi-citizens. The two are hardly ever in a zero-sum game, but both need representation even if they are.

3. QUASI-CITIZENS IN THE COMMUNITY ARE REPRESENTED

1. In the large literature on the varied meanings and methods of citizenship, some more interesting considerations are emerging from the effort to describe and prescribe the various meaning of "citizenship" in the European Union. See, for example, A. Lansbergen and J. Shaw, "National Membership Models in a Multilevel Europe," *International Journal of Constitutional Law* 8, no. 1 (2010): 50–71.

2. C. M. Rodriguez, "Noncitizen Voting and the Extraconstitutional Construction of the Polity," *International Journal of Constitutional Law* 8, no. 1 (2010): 30–49.

3. The number of noncitizens in a all countries is considerable. Although counting them is difficult for many reasons, such as illegality and temporary residency, a reasonable estimate is that 10 percent of the people in the United States are noncitizens.

4. A. O. Hirschman, *Exit, Voice, and Loyalty: Responses to Decline in Firms, Organizations, and States* (Cambridge, Mass.: Harvard University Press, 1970).

4. QUASI-CITIZENS IN OTHER JURISDICTIONS ARE REPRESENTED

1. The parallel with "intelligence"—for example, through agencies such as the CIA in the United States—is good because it emphasizes the need for ongoing connections, but it breaks down with regard to the sanctions that people have to be able to use in order to make the links democratically workable.

2. See, for example, the discussion of "overlapping legal systems" in R. A. Schapiro, "In the Twilight of the Nation-State: Subnational Constitutions in the New World Order," *Rutgers Law Journal* 39, no. 4 (2008): 801–836. According to Shapiro,

> At one point, theories of sovereignty focused on two distinct sets of relationships: the relationship between a nation-state and other nation-states and the relationship of a nation-state to domestic sub-national entities, such as cities and localities. While the former relationship was among equals, the latter was a relationship of the dominant authority with subordinates. Globalization has transformed these two distinct pairs of relationships into a single relationship among localities, their nation-states, and the international legal order. (814)

3. The image of singular, coherent nation-states is perpetuated in popular and media discourse when people speak of "Mexico's positions on immigration" or "Pakistan's position on the war on terror," as if there were not only no differences of opinion about those issues among the citizens of those countries, but no connection between factions or groups within those countries and international groups in regard to those issues.

4. A.-M. Slaughter, *A New World Order* (Princeton, N.J.: Princeton University Press, 2004). For influences of social movements, see M. E. Keck and K. Sikkink, *Activists Beyond Borders: Advocacy Networks in International Politics* (Ithaca, N.Y.: Cornell University Press, 1998).

5. There is a wealth of conceptually rich analysis of the European Union and what would constitute democracy at the EU level, and the reciprocal question of how to link European-wide interests with the politics any one country. For a sample of the sorts of analyses under way, see G. Majone, "Europe's 'Democratic Deficit': The Question of Standards," *European Law Journal* 4, no. 1 (1998): 5–28.

6. The quasi-citizens of occupied countries also try to hold decision makers accountable. Their methods range from noncooperation, through passive resistance, to terror and assassination. Again, these means are also used by domestic groups, although the coercive aspect of the occupation no doubt shifts the balance toward violent forms of action. See F. Fanon, *The Wretched of the Earth*, trans. Richard Philcox (New York: Grove Press, 2004).

5. CONNECTING PEOPLE AND DECISION MAKERS

1. Famously, in J. A. Schumpeter, *Capitalism, Socialism, and Democracy* (New York: Harper & Row, 1975).

2. Students of different types of representation usually include one that does not involve links. P. Pettit makes the distinction between "indicative" and "responsive" representation in "Varieties of Political Representation," in *Political Representation*, ed. I. Shapiro, S. C. Stokes, E. J. Wood, and A. S. Kirshner (Cambridge: Cambridge University Press, 2009), 61–89. J. Mansbridge includes "gyroscopic" with similar intent in "Rethinking Representation," *American Political Science Review* 97, no. 4 (2003): 515–528.

3. "Representation" is treated this way by both the original defenders and the original critics of the Constitution in A. Hamilton, J. Madison, and J. Jay, *The Federalist Papers*, ed. C. Rossiter (1787–1788; New York: Signet Classics, 2003).

6. ORGANIZATIONS AND THEIR ALLIANCES CHANGE RAPIDLY

1. J.-J. Rousseau, in formulating his idea of the General Will of the people, condemned all "partial societies," famously assuming that all the people should come together without prior discussion, in *On the Social Contract*, trans. G. D. H. Cole (1762; Mineola, N.Y.: Dover, 2003), chap. 3. Local or neighborhood communities and associations frequently frown on factions.

2. For ways to deal with groups that undercut democracy, which they identify as the "mischiefs of faction," see J. Cohen and J. Rogers, eds., *Associations and Democracy* (London: Verso, 1995).

3. To describe new sorts of groups, I have argued, there are really four possible negatives involved: nongovernmental, nonparty, nonprofit, and nonfamilial. See D. A. Chalmers, "What Is It About Associations in Civil Society That Promotes Democracy?" (http://www.columbia.edu/~chalmers /AssocDem.html). But here we are being inclusive.

4. A. Hamilton, J. Madison, and J. Jay, *The Federalist Papers*, ed. C. Rossiter (1787–1788; New York: Signet Classics, 2003), no. 10.

5. A. de Tocqueville, *Democracy in America and Two Essays on America*, trans. G. E. Bevan, ed. I. Kramnick (1835; London: Penguin, 2003), bk. 2.

6. On social capital, see, especially, R. D. Putnam, R. Leonardi, and R. Y. Nanetti, *Making Democracy Work: Civic Traditions in Modern Italy* (Princeton, N.J.: Princeton University Press, 1994).

7. Most obviously in *The Communist Manifesto*.

8. This perspective was commonly associated with A. F. Bentley, *The Process of Government: A Study of Social Pressures* (Chicago: University of Chicago Press, 1908); D. B. Truman, *The Governmental Process: Political Interests and Public Opinion* (New York: Knopf, 1951); and R. A. Dahl, *Who Governs? Democracy and Power in an American City* (New Haven, Conn.: Yale University Press, 1961).

9. This is the approach developed as "associative democracy" in J. Cohen and J. Rogers, "Secondary Associations and Democratic Governance," in *Associations and Democracy*, ed. Cohen and Rogers, 7–98.

10. This is the subject of much discussion, which is summarized in A. Fung, "Associations and Democracy: Between Theories, Hopes, and Realities," *Annual Review of Sociology* 29 (2003): 515–539.

11. Although the term "revolution" is commonly applied to the impact of digital technology on communication, it is more like a snowball rolling down a mountain, growing larger and heavier and gaining speed as it goes.

12. B. A. Bimber, *Information and American Democracy: Technology in the Evolution of Political Power* (Cambridge: Cambridge University Press, 2003).

13. C. R. Sunstein makes the argument about the rich choices leading to fragmentation in *Republic.com 2.0* (Princeton, N.J.: Princeton University Press, 2007). Summary efforts to assess the impact of digital communication

are probably a thing of the past, because the effects have been so widespread and, as many would argue, more in the direction of modifying and supplementing than transforming. A good summary of the thinking a decade ago can be found in P. DiMaggio et al., "Social Implications of the Internet," *Annual Review of Sociology* 27 (2001): 307–336.

14. One small piece of this story is the impact of "blogs" on helping to shape public debate. See H. Farrell and D. W. Drezner, "The Power and Politics of Blogs," *Public Choice* 134, nos. 1–2 (2008): 15–30; and, on reaching new publics, D. Woodly, "New Competencies in Democratic Communication? Blogs, Agenda Setting and Political Participation," *Public Choice* 134, nos. 1–2 (2008): 109–123.

7. PERSONAL NETWORKS ARE IMPORTANT

1. The current critical use of the word "earmarks" in American politics expresses the feeling that something done for "one's own"—in this sense, one's own community—is somehow illegitimate. Despite this sentiment, politicians who have done much for their constituents often are lauded—as was, for example, Senator Robert Byrd of West Virginia.

2. Part of this dominant negativity in the literature lies in the preoccupation of many scholars of personal ties with the role of connections in electoral politics, where it seems contrary to the ideal of a vote cast for a principle or even a group interest. See the excellent article by H. Kitschelt, "Linkages Between Citizens and Politicians in Democratic Polities," *Comparative Political Studies* 33, nos. 6–7 (2000): 845–879.

3. Sorting out the various meanings of "policy network" can be daunting. See G. Jordan, "Sub-Governments, Policy Communities and Networks: Refilling the Old Bottles?" *Journal of Theoretical Politics* 2, no. 3 (1990): 319–338.

4. A survey of network theory's application to political analysis (as well as social analysis) found that networks were often identified as crucial in policy innovation and agenda setting. See F. S. Berry et al., "Three Traditions of Network Research: What the Public Management Research Agenda Can Learn from Other Research Communities," *Public Administration Review* 64, no. 5 (2004): 539–552. Whether networks make a difference on issues beyond personal domination has been a long-standing dispute. An interesting empirical analysis is M. Howlett, "Do Networks

Matter? Linking Policy Network Structure to Policy Outcomes: Evidence from Four Canadian Policy Sectors, 1990–2000," *Canadian Journal of Political Science / Revue canadienne de science politique* 35 (2002): 235–267.

5. It has been suggested that the new interdependence of nations on coordination of policy might rely on personal networks. See W. D. Coleman and A. Perl, "Internationalized Policy Environments and Policy Network Analysis," *Political Studies* 47, no. 4 (1999): 691–709.

6. D. A. Chalmers, S. B. Martin, and K. Piester, "Associative Networks: New Structures of Representation for the Popular Sectors?" in *The New Politics of Inequality in Latin America: Rethinking Participation and Representation*, ed. D. A. Chalmers et al. (Oxford: Oxford University Press, 1997), 543–582.

7. Among others, see the early work of F. H. Cardoso, *Empresário industrial e desenvolvimento econômico no Brasil* (São Paulo: Difusão Européia do Livro, 1964).

8. R. K. Merton, *Social Theory and Social Structure* (Glencoe, Ill.: Free Press, 1957), chap. 3.

9. An example of such networks is the Committees of Correspondence, which emerged before the American Revolution to coordinate actions within and between the colonies against the British government and became a path toward developing the new institutions.

8. LAW- AND POLICY MAKING

1. J. S. Mill, a famous proponent of free, even erroneous, speech and a firm believer in the ability of the gentlemen who would come together in the legislature, did not provide a breakdown of the parts of that conversation in *On Liberty and Other Essays*, ed. J. Gray (Oxford: Oxford University Press, 2008).

9. DELIBERATION IS AS IMPORTANT AS BARGAINING

1. "Data, theories, and interpretations" is my shorthand for the cognitive elements that may come into play in the course of deliberation. It at least gives a wide field for the "cognitive." I will use the word "information" to refer to all three.

2. For one analysis of the relationship of these elements, considering how practical bargaining can turn into deliberation, see P. McLaverty and D. Halpin, "Deliberative Drift: The Emergence of Deliberation in the Policy Process," *International Political Science Review* 29, no. 2 (2008): 197–214.

3. Such bargaining has become very important in explanatory theory because of the way it fits into rational choice theory, so important in economics. It has a long history in political science as well, traceable to the liberal view of the political system's relationship with a market-like population. For its relationship with deliberation, see J. Bohman and W. Rehg, eds., *Deliberative Democracy: Essays on Reason and Politics* (Cambridge, Mass.: MIT Press, 1997), particularly the chapter by Jon Elster, "The Market and the Forum: Three Varieties of Political Theory," 3–34.

4. A classic formulation is H. D. Lasswell, *Politics: Who Gets What, When, How. With Postscript (1958)* (1936; New York: Meridian Books, 1958).

5. The term "debate" is often used to suggest deliberation—as in legislators' debate over dealing with debt limits or "the public debate over gay marriage"—but it has been turned into something quite different. The public show-and-tell confrontations often called "debates" in legislatures, on television, and on public platforms—assuming that they are intended to contribute to the deliberation at all—are undertaken not to seek the best solution to a problem, but to let some set of others (the audience, the voters, the decision makers) contemplate, weigh the evidence and the arguments, and choose one proposition. Deliberation takes place after the debate—if at all.

6. In presidential systems, of course, the legislative process includes the president.

7. Some advocates of democratic deliberation argue that elections can become more deliberative if the people are more engaged. See, for example, the suggestion for a "deliberation day" in B. A. Ackerman and J. S. Fishkin, *Deliberation Day* (New Haven, Conn.: Yale University Press, 2004). But while discussions among voters may increase their sophistication, it is a long step to making the national decision process more deliberative.

8. Jürgen Habermas had been followed by many modern theorists in making this point. See C. Calhoun, ed., *Habermas and the Public Sphere* (Cambridge, Mass.: MIT Press, 1992). For a provocative link between the constitution of "public spheres" and inequality, see N. Fraser, "Rethinking the Public Sphere: A Contribution to the Critique of Actually Existing

Democracy," *Social Text* 25–26 (1990): 56–80, reprinted in *Habermas and the Public Sphere*, ed. Calhoun, 109–142.

9. In a change of ideas given a strong boost by H. de Soto, in collaboration with Instituto Libertad y Democracia, *The Other Path: The Invisible Revolution in the Third World* (New York: Harper & Row, 1989).

10. Marx sought to promote such a transformation through knowledge, by converting the great miscellany of workers into proletarians with a historic political mission.

10. DECISIONS ARE MADE IN MULTIPLE VENUES

1. In analyzing decision making in administrative practice, the idea of multiple venues is common, as in the "garbage can" model of decision making. The goal of that model, however, seems to be to explain the decisions that are made, not identify the institutions that might improve the making of decisions. See J. Bendor, T. M. Moe, and K. W. Shotts, "Recycling the Garbage Can: An Assessment of the Research Program," *American Political Science Review* 95, no. 1 (2001): 169–190.

2. There are many variations. For differences in the distribution of powers, see A. C. Stepan, "Federalism and Democracy: Beyond the U.S. Model," *Journal of Democracy* 10, no. 4 (1999): 19–34.

3. For a different perspective, but similar conclusions about cross-national decision venues, see A.-M. Slaughter, *A New World Order* (Princeton, N.J.: Princeton University Press, 2004).

4. For one example among many, see G. Majone, "Europe's 'Democratic Deficit': The Question of Standards," *European Law Journal* 4, no. 1 (1998): 5–28.

5. They are "ad hoc" in the sense that they are formed for a particular purpose, not in the more colloquial meaning of "slapdash" or "casual."

6. For a dramatic view of this multiplicity of border crossings driven by the expansion of digital communication and leading to a redefinition of the state, see R. Ronfeldt and D. Varda, "The Prospects for Cyberocracy (Revisited)," 2008, Social Science Research Network (http://ssrn.com /abstract=1325809). Another related view, emphasizing the non-state-controlled "private networks," can be found in S. Sassen, "Digital Networks and the State: Some Governance Questions," *Theory, Culture & Society* 17, no. 4 (2000): 19–33.

7. It is symptomatic of the state of conceptualization of representative institutions that discussions of the way in which government agencies relate to the people electronically often have focused on the way they deliver services, rather than gathering information about citizens' preferences, circumstances, and suggestions. Thus they ignore the potential input into the communication necessary for representation. See, for example, J. E. Fountain, "The Virtual State: Transforming American Government?" *National Civic Review* 90, no. 3 (2001): 241–251. More recently, analysts are defining the new electronic links as two-way. The British experience is discussed in J. Morison, "Gov 2.0: Towards a User Generated State?" *Modern Law Review* 73, no. 4 (2010): 551–577. There is also considerable interest in "electronic rule making," which involves processing citizens' opinions in the shaping of regulatory rules. See S. W. D. Shulman et al., "Electronic Rulemaking: A Public Participation Research Agenda for the Social Sciences," *Social Science Computer Review* 21, no. 2 (2003): 162–178.

8. An interesting effort to harmonize the multiplicity of venues with the standards of deliberative democracy can be found in J. Mansbridge, "The Deliberative System Disaggregated," American Political Science Association 2010 Annual Meeting Paper.

9. One approach to this multiplicity is to adopt a normative principle of deliberative democracy and make each decision network "directly deliberative," as is done in J. Cohen and C. Sabel, "Directly-Deliberative Polyarchy," *European Law Journal* 3, no. 4 (1997): 313–342. Similar to recommendations for "deliberative democracy," the aim seems to be getting everyone actively involved in the final decision making. It renders the vision utopian. The use of Robert Dahl's term "polyarchy" does move in the right direction, however. See R. A. Dahl, *Polyarchy: Participation and Opposition* (New Haven, Conn.: Yale University Press, 1971).

CONCLUSION

1. Ignoring troublesome details is a common practice in the social and policy sciences, reflected in such major "as if" assumptions as the notion that actions can be understood as rational in order to maximize their utility. See the classic argument in M. Friedman, *Essays in Positive Economics* (Chicago: University of Chicago Press, 1953). The problems arise when the troublesome details become, like the six facts discussed in this book, too big to ignore.

2. J. Habermas, *Between Facts and Norms: Contributions to a Discourse Theory of Law and Democracy*, trans. William Rehg (Cambridge: Polity Press, 1996).

3. Habermas is the chief source, but see also the discussion of the requirements for "public reason" in J. Rawls, "The Idea of Public Reason Revisited," *University of Chicago Law Review* 64 (1997): 765–807. See also S. Macedo, "Why Public Reason? Citizens' Reasons and the Constitution of the Public Sphere," 2010, Social Science Research Network (http://ssrn.com/abstract=1664085).

4. Among the most prominent advocates for a democratization of deliberation, as opposed to analyzing the need to realize democracy when deliberation is, in fact, taking place, is J. S. Dryzek, *Discursive Democracy: Politics, Policy, and Political Science* (Cambridge: Cambridge University Press, 1990). There have been many discussions of "democratic deliberation" in practice. For one example, see E. F. Einsiedel and D. L. Eastlick, "Consensus Conferences as Deliberative Democracy: A Communications Perspective," *Science Communication* 21, no. 4 (2000): 323–343.

5. See, for example, the suggestion for a "deliberation day" in B. A. Ackerman and J. S. Fishkin, *Deliberation Day* (New Haven, Conn.: Yale University Press, 2004).

6. A critique of deliberation that depends on its being taken as a program for involving people in decisions is L. Sanders, "Against Deliberation," *Political Theory* 25, no. 3 (1997): 347–376.

7. One intriguing example, among many, is M. R. Harris, "Environmental Deliberative Democracy and the Search for Administrative Legitimacy: A Legal Positivism Approach," *University of Michigan Journal of Law Reform* 44, no. 2 (2011): 343–382.

8. For an interesting example of an effort to specify what is needed for political choice, see E. Ostrom and V. Ostrom, "The Quest for Meaning in Public Choice," *American Journal of Economics and Sociology* 63, no. 1 (2004): 105–147.

9. Some might say that every core citizen, every human being on this ecologically fragile planet, and every voter who will be called on to hold the decision makers accountable has a stake in the outcome and has the right and duty to participate. But building decision networks is a practical problem, involving choices about the people who are significantly affected and those who are peripheral.

WORKS CITED

Ackerman, B. A., and J. S. Fishkin. *Deliberation Day*. New Haven, Conn.: Yale University Press, 2004.

Anderson, B. R. O. G.. *Imagined Communities: Reflections on the Origin and Spread of Nationalism*. London: Verso, 2006.

Armijo, L. E., P. Faucher, and M. Dembinska. "Compared to What? Assessing Brazil's Political Institutions." *Comparative Political Studies* 39, no. 6 (2006): 759–786.

Bauböck, R. "Global Justice, Freedom of Movement and Democratic Citizenship." *European Journal of Sociology / Archives européennes de sociologie* 50, no. 1 (2009): 1–31.

———. "Stakeholder Citizenship and Transnational Political Participation: A Normative Evaluation of External Voting." *Fordham Law Review* 75, no. 5 (2007): 2393–2447.

Bellamy, R. "Democracy Without Democracy? Can the EU's Democratic 'Outputs' Be Separated from the Democratic 'Inputs' Provided by Competitive Parties and Majority Rule?" *Journal of European Public Policy* 17, no. 1 (2010): 2–19.

Bendor, J., T. M. Moe, and K. W. Shotts. "Recycling the Garbage Can: An Assessment of the Research Program." *American Political Science Review* 95, no. 1 (2001): 169–190.

Bentley, A. F. *The Process of Government: A Study of Social Pressures.*
Chicago: University of Chicago Press, 1908.

Berry, F. S., R. S. Brower, S. O. Choi, W. X. Goa, E. Jang, M. Kwon, and J.
Word. "Three Traditions of Network Research: What the Public Management Research Agenda Can Learn from Other Research Communities." *Public Administration Review* 64, no. 5 (2004): 539–552.

Bimber, B. A. *Information and American Democracy: Technology in the Evolution of Political Power.* Cambridge: Cambridge University Press, 2003.

Bohman, J., and W. Rehg, eds. *Deliberative Democracy: Essays on Reason
and Politics.* Cambridge, Mass.: MIT Press, 1997.

Burke, E. *Reflections on the Revolution in France.* 1790. Oxford: Oxford
University Press, 2009.

Calhoun, C., ed. *Habermas and the Public Sphere.* Cambridge, Mass.: MIT
Press, 1992.

Cardoso, F. H. *Empresário industrial e desenvolvimento econômico no Brasil.* São Paulo: Difusão Européia do Livro, 1964.

Chalmers, D. A. "What Is It About Associations in Civil Society That Promotes Democracy?" http://www.columbia.edu/~chalmers/AssocDem.
html.

Chalmers, D. A., S. B. Martin, and K. Piester, "Associative Networks: New
Structures of Representation for the Popular Sectors?" In *The New Politics of Inequality in Latin America: Rethinking Participation and Representation,* edited by D. A. Chalmers, C. M. Vilas, K. Hite, S. B. Martin, K.
Piester, and M. Segarra, 543–582. Oxford: Oxford University Press, 1997.

Cohen, E. F. *Semi-Citizenship in Democratic Politics.* New York: Cambridge
University Press, 2009.

Cohen, J., and J. Rogers. "Secondary Associations and Democratic Governance." In *Associations and Democracy,* ed. J. Cohen and J. Rogers,
7–98. London: Verso, 1995.

Cohen, J., and C. Sabel. "Directly-Deliberative Polyarchy." *European Law
Journal* 3, no. 4 (1997): 313–342.

Cohen, J. L. "Changing Paradigms of Citizenship and the Exclusiveness of
the Demos." *International Sociology* 14, no. 3 (1999): 245–268.

Coleman, W. D., and A. Perl. "Internationalized Policy Environments and
Policy Network Analysis." *Political Studies* 47, no. 4 (1999): 691–709.

Dahl, R. A. *Polyarchy: Participation and Opposition.* New Haven, Conn.:
Yale University Press, 1971.

——. *Who Governs? Democracy and Power in an American City.* New Haven, Conn.: Yale University Press, 1961.

DiMaggio, P., E. Hargittai, W. R. Neuman, and J. P. Robinson. "Social Implications of the Internet." *Annual Review of Sociology* 27 (2001): 307–336.

Disch, L. "Rethinking Responsiveness." Western Political Science Association 2010 Annual Meeting Paper. Social Science Research Network, http://ssrn.com/abstract=1580937.

Dryzek, J. S. *Discursive Democracy: Politics, Policy, and Political Science.* Cambridge: Cambridge University Press, 1990.

Einsiedel, E. F., and D. L. Eastlick. "Consensus Conferences as Deliberative Democracy: A Communications Perspective." *Science Communication* 21, no. 4 (2000): 323–343.

Fanon, F. *The Wretched of the Earth.* Translated by Richard Philcox. New York: Grove Press, 2004.

Farrell, H., and D. W. Drezner. "The Power and Politics of Blogs." *Public Choice* 134, nos. 1–2 (2008): 15–30.

Fountain, J. E. "The Virtual State: Transforming American Government?" *National Civic Review* 90, no. 3 (2001): 241–251.

Fraser, N. "Rethinking the Public Sphere: A Contribution to the Critique of Actually Existing Democracy." *Social Text* 25–26 (1990): 56–80.

Friedman, M. *Essays in Positive Economics.* Chicago: University of Chicago Press, 1953.

Fung, A. "Associations and Democracy: Between Theories, Hopes, and Realities." *Annual Review of Sociology* 29 (2003): 515–539.

Goodin, R. E. "Representing Diversity." *British Journal of Political Science* 34, no. 3 (2004): 453–468.

Habermas, J. *Between Facts and Norms: Contributions to a Discourse Theory of Law and Democracy.* Translated by William Rehg. Cambridge: Polity Press, 1996.

Hamilton, A., J. Madison, and J. Jay. *The Federalist Papers.* Edited by C. Rossiter. 1787–1788. New York: Signet Classics, 2003.

Harris, M. R. "Environmental Deliberative Democracy and the Search for Administrative Legitimacy: A Legal Positivism Approach." *University of Michigan Journal of Law Reform* 44, no. 2 (2011): 343–382.

Hirschman, A. O. *Exit, Voice, and Loyalty: Responses to Decline in Firms, Organizations, and States.* Cambridge, Mass.: Harvard University Press, 1970.

Howlett, M. "Do Networks Matter? Linking Policy Network Structure to Policy Outcomes: Evidence from Four Canadian Policy Sectors, 1990–2000." *Canadian Journal of Political Science / Revue canadienne de science politique* 35 (2002): 235–267.

Jordan, G. "Sub-Governments, Policy Communities and Networks: Refilling the Old Bottles?" *Journal of Theoretical Politics* 2, no. 3 (1990): 319–338.

Keck, M. E., and K. Sikkink. *Activists Beyond Borders: Advocacy Networks in International Politics.* Ithaca, N.Y.: Cornell University Press, 1998.

Kingdon, J. W. *Agendas, Alternatives, and Public Policies.* New York: Longman, 2003.

Kitschelt, H. "Linkages Between Citizens and Politicians in Democratic Polities." *Comparative Political Studies* 33, nos. 6–7 (2000): 845–879.

Lansbergen, A., and J. Shaw. "National Membership Models in a Multilevel Europe." *International Journal of Constitutional Law* 8, no. 1 (2010): 50–71.

Lasswell, H. D. *Politics: Who Gets What, When, How. With Postscript (1958).* 1936. New York: Meridian Books, 1958.

Locke, J. *Second Treatise of Government.* Edited by C. B. Macpherson. 1690. Indianapolis: Hackett, 1980.

Macedo, S. "Why Public Reason? Citizens' Reasons and the Constitution of the Public Sphere." 2010. Social Science Research Network, http://ssrn.com/abstract=1664085.

Majone, G. "Europe's 'Democratic Deficit': The Question of Standards." *European Law Journal* 4, no. 1 (1998): 5–28.

Mansbridge, J. "The Deliberative System Disaggregated." American Political Science Association 2010 Annual Meeting Paper.

———. "Rethinking Representation." *American Political Science Review* 97, no. 4 (2003): 515–528.

McLaverty, P., and D. Halpin. "Deliberative Drift: The Emergence of Deliberation in the Policy Process." *International Political Science Review* 29, no. 2 (2008): 197–214.

Merton, R. K. *Social Theory and Social Structure.* Glencoe, Ill.: Free Press, 1957.

Mill, J. S. *On Liberty and Other Essays.* Edited by J. Gray. Oxford: Oxford University Press, 2008.

Morison, J. "Gov 2.0: Towards a User Generated State?" *Modern Law Review* 73, no. 4 (2010): 551–577.

Ostrom, E., and V. Ostrom. "The Quest for Meaning in Public Choice." *American Journal of Economics and Sociology* 63, no. 1 (2004): 105–147.

Peruzzotti, E. "Constituents, Representatives and the Dual Politics of Democratic Representation." 2009. Social Science Research Network, http://ssrn.com/abstract=1653510.

Pettit, P. "Varieties of Political Representation." In *Political Representation*, edited by I. Shapiro, S. C. Stokes, E. J. Wood, and A. S. Kirshner, 61–89. Cambridge: Cambridge University Press, 2009.

Pitkin, H. F. *The Concept of Representation*. Berkeley: University of California Press, 1967.

Putnam, R. D., R. Leonardi, and R. Y. Nanetti. *Making Democracy Work: Civic Traditions in Modern Italy*. Princeton, N.J.: Princeton University Press, 1994.

Rawls, J. "The Idea of Public Reason Revisited." *University of Chicago Law Review* 64 (1997): 765–807.

Rodriguez, C. M. "Noncitizen Voting and the Extraconstitutional Construction of the Polity." *International Journal of Constitutional Law* 8, no. 1 (2010): 30–49.

Ronfeldt, R., and D. Varda. "The Prospects for Cyberocracy (Revisited)." 2008. Social Science Research Network, http://ssrn.com/abstract=1325809.

Rousseau, J.-J. *On the Social Contract*. Translated by G. D. H. Cole. 1762. Mineola, N.Y.: Dover, 2003.

Sanders, L. "Against Deliberation." *Political Theory* 25, no. 3 (1997): 347–376.

Sassen, S. "Digital Networks and the State: Some Governance Questions." *Theory, Culture & Society* 17, no. 4 (2000): 19–33.

Schapiro, R. A. "In the Twilight of the Nation-State: Subnational Constitutions in the New World Order." *Rutgers Law Journal* 39, no. 4 (2008): 801–836.

Schmitter, P. C., and T. L. Karl. "What Democracy Is . . . and Is Not." *Journal of Democracy* 2, no. 4 (1991): 75–88.

Schmitter, P. C., and G. Lehmbruch. *Trends Toward Corporatist Intermediation*. Beverly Hills, Calif.: Sage, 1979.

Schumpeter, J. A. *Capitalism, Socialism, and Democracy*. New York: Harper & Row, 1975.

Shulman, S. W., D. Schlosberg, S. Zavestoski, and D. Courard-Hauri. "Electronic Rulemaking: A Public Participation Research Agenda for the

Social Sciences." *Social Science Computer Review* 21, no. 2 (2003): 162–178.

Sieyès, E. J. *What Is the Third Estate?* New York: Praeger, 1964.

Slaughter, A.-M. *A New World Order.* Princeton, N.J.: Princeton University Press, 2004.

Soto, H. de, in collaboration with Instituto Libertad y Democracia. *The Other Path: The Invisible Revolution in the Third World.* New York: Harper & Row, 1989.

Stepan, A. C. "Federalism and Democracy: Beyond the U.S. Model." *Journal of Democracy* 10, no. 4 (1999): 19–34.

Stepan, A., and G. B. Robertson. "An 'Arab' More Than 'Muslim' Electoral Gap." *Journal of Democracy* 14, no. 3 (2003): 30–44.

Sunstein, C. R. *Republic.com 2.0.* Princeton, N.J.: Princeton University Press, 2007.

Tarrow, S. G. *Power in Movement: Social Movements and Contentious Politics.* Cambridge: Cambridge University Press, 1998.

Tilly, C., and S. G. Tarrow. *Contentious Politics.* Boulder, Colo.: Paradigm, 2007.

Tocqueville, A. de. *Democracy in America and Two Essays on America.* Translated by G. E. Bevan. Edited by I. Kramnick. 1835. London: Penguin, 2003.

Truman, D. B. *The Governmental Process: Political Interests and Public Opinion.* New York: Knopf, 1951.

Urbinati, N., and M. E. Warren. "The Concept of Representation in Contemporary Democratic Theory." *Annual Review of Political Science* 11 (2008): 387–412.

Weber, M. *The Methodology of the Social Sciences.* Edited and translated by E. A. Shils and H. A. Finch. 1903–1917. New York: Free Press, 1997.

Woodly, D. "New Competencies in Democratic Communication? Blogs, Agenda Setting and Political Participation." *Public Choice* 134, nos. 1–2 (2008): 109–123.

Suggested Readings

The recent awareness of the gap between the models of democratic institutions we use and the reality of the political activity that shapes the outcome of policy making have produced a wide-ranging set of analyses, reconceptualizations, theoretical speculations, and exploratory studies. The following is an eclectic list of some efforts that I have found stimulating, roughly grouped according to the concepts that play a role in this book.

WAYS OF CONCEPTUALIZING DEMOCRACY

Armijo, L. E., P. Faucher, and M. Dembinska. "Compared to What? Assessing Brazil's Political Institutions." *Comparative Political Studies* 39, no. 6 (2006): 759–786.

Dahl, R. A. *Democracy and Its Critics.* New Haven, Conn.: Yale University Press, 1989.

Fraser, N. "Rethinking the Public Sphere: A Contribution to the Critique of Actually Existing Democracy." *Social Text* 25–26 (1990): 56–80.

Scharpf, F. W. *Governing in Europe: Effective and Democratic?* Oxford: Oxford University Press, 1999.

REPRESENTATION

Brito Vieira, M., and D. Runciman. *Representation*. Cambridge: Polity Press, 2008.

Disch, L. "Rethinking Responsiveness." Western Political Science Association 2010 Annual Meeting Paper. Social Science Research Network, http://ssrn.com/abstract=1580937.

Goodin, R. E. "Representing Diversity." *British Journal of Political Science* 34, no. 3 (2004): 453–468.

Mansbridge, J. "Rethinking Representation." *American Political Science Review* 97, no. 4 (2003): 515–528

——. "Should Blacks Represent Blacks and Women Represent Women? A Contingent 'Yes'." *Journal of Politics* 61, no. 3 (1999): 628–657.

Rehfeld, A. "Towards a General Theory of Political Representation." *Journal of Politics* 68, no. 1 (2006): 1–21.

Saward, M. *The Representative Claim*. Oxford: Oxford University Press, 2010.

Shapiro, I., S. C. Stokes, E. J. Wood, and A. S. Kirshner, eds. *Political Representation*. Cambridge: Cambridge University Press, 2009.

Urbinati, N. *Representative Democracy: Principles and Genealogy*. Chicago: University of Chicago Press, 2006.

Urbinati, N., and M. E. Warren. "The Concept of Representation in Contemporary Democratic Theory." *Annual Review of Political Science* 11 (2008): 387–412.

Young, I. M. *Inclusion and Democracy*. New York: Oxford University Press, 2002.

CITIZENS AND QUASI-CITIZENS

Barnes, M., J. Newman, A Knops, and H. Sullivan. "Constituting 'the Public' in Public Participation." *Public Administration* 81, no. 2 (2003): 379–399.

Bauböck, R. "Stakeholder Citizenship and Transnational Political Participation: A Normative Evaluation of External Voting." *Fordham Law Review* 75, no. 5 (2007): 2393–2447.

Canovan, M. *The People*. Cambridge: Polity Press, 2005.

Cohen, E. F. *Semi-Citizenship in Democratic Politics*. New York: Cambridge University Press, 2009.

Cohen, J. L. "Changing Paradigms of Citizenship and the Exclusiveness of the Demos." *International Sociology* 14, no. 3 (1999): 245–268.

Kymlicka, W. *Multicultural Odysseys: Navigating the New International Politics of Diversity*. Oxford: Oxford University Press, 2007.

MacKenzie, M. K. "Future Publics: Democracy, Deliberation, and Long-Term Decision-Making." American Political Science Association 2010 Annual Meeting Paper.

Mindus, P. "Europeanisation of Citizenship Within the EU: Perspectives and Ambiguities." 2010. Jean Monnet Working Papers (European Centre of Excellence–Trento). Social Science Research Network, http://ssrn .com/abstract=1616722.

Schapiro, R. A. "In the Twilight of the Nation-State: Subnational Constitutions in the New World Order." *Rutgers Law Journal* 39, no. 4 (2008): 801–836.

Tierney, S. *Accommodating Cultural Diversity*. Aldershot, Eng · Ashgate, 2007.

Tuschhoff, C. "The Compounding Effect: The Impact of Federalism on the Concept of Representation." *West European Politics* 22, no. 2 (1999): 16–33.

PERSONAL NETWORKS AND CIVIL SOCIETY

Berry, F. S., R. S. Brower, S. O. Choi, W. X. Goa, E. Jang, M. Kwon, and J. Word. "Three Traditions of Network Research: What the Public Management Research Agenda Can Learn from Other Research Communities." *Public Administration Review* 64, no. 5 (2004): 539–552.

Kitschelt, H. "Linkages Between Citizens and Politicians in Democratic Polities." *Comparative Political Studies* 33, nos. 6–7 (2000): 845–879.

Warren, M. E. "What Does Corruption Mean in a Democracy?" *American Journal of Political Science* 48, no. 2 (2004): 328–343.

DELIBERATION AND INFORMATION

Aaken, A. van, C. List, and C. Luetge. *Deliberation and Decision: Economics, Constitutional Theory and Deliberative Democracy.* Aldershot, Eng: Ashgate, 2004.

Anderson, E. "The Epistemology of Democracy." *Episteme: A Journal of Social Epistemology* 3, nos. 1–2 (2006): 8–22.

Bohman, J., and W. Rehg. *Deliberative Democracy: Essays on Reason and Politics.* Cambridge, Mass.: MIT Press, 1997.

Brown, M. B. "Fairly Balanced: The Politics of Representation on Government Advisory Committees." *Political Research Quarterly* 61, no. 4 (2008): 547–560.

Gutmann, A., and D. F. Thompson. *Democracy and Disagreement.* Cambridge, Mass.: Belknap Press of Harvard University Press, 1996.

Head, B. "Evidence-based Policy: Principles and Requirements." In *Strengthening Evidence-based Policy in the Australian Federation.* Vol. 1, *Proceedings,* 13–26. Melbourne: Productivity Commission, 2010.

Jasanoff, S. *The Fifth Branch: Science Advisers as Policymakers.* Cambridge, Mass.: Harvard University Press, 1990.

Kingdon, J. W. *Agendas, Alternatives, and Public Policies.* New York: Longman, 2003.

Lentsch, J., and P. Weingart, eds. *The Politics of Scientific Advice: Institutional Design for Quality Assurance.* Cambridge: Cambridge University Press, 2011.

Maasen, S., and P. Weingart. *Democratization of Expertise? Exploring Novel Forms of Scientific Advice in Political Decision-Making.* Dordrecht: Springer, 2005.

Mansbridge, J. "The Deliberative System Disaggregated." American Political Science Association 2010 Annual Meeting Paper.

McLaverty, P., and D. Halpin. "Deliberative Drift: The Emergence of Deliberation in the Policy Process." *International Political Science Review* 29, no. 2 (2008): 197–214.

McQuide, B. S. "Competitive Informational Lobbying in Congress: Can Citizen Groups Compete on New Policy Issues?" Western Political Science Association 2010 Annual Meeting Paper. Social Science Research Network, http://ssrn.com/abstract=1580603.

Pielke, R. A. *The Honest Broker: Making Sense of Science in Policy and Politics.* Cambridge: Cambridge University Press, 2007.

Rawls, J. "The Idea of Public Reason Revisited." *University of Chicago Law Review* 64 (1997): 765–807.

DECISION NETWORKS

Bendor, J., T. M. Moe, and K. W. Shotts. "Recycling the Garbage Can: An Assessment of the Research Program." *American Political Science Review* 95, no. 1 (200): 169–190.

Coleman, W. D., and A. Perl. "Internationalized Policy Environments and Policy Network Analysis." *Political Studies* 47, no. 4 (1999): 691–709.

Howlett, M. "Do Networks Matter? Linking Policy Network Structure to Policy Outcomes: Evidence from Four Canadian Policy Sectors, 1990–2000." *Canadian Journal of Political Science / Revue canadienne de science politique* 35 (2002): 235–267.

Jordan, G. "Sub-Governments, Policy Communities and Networks: Refilling the Old Bottles?" *Journal of Theoretical Politics* 2, no. 3 (1990): 319–338.

Marsh, D., and M. Smith. "Understanding Policy Networks: Towards a Dialectical Approach." *Political Studies* 48, no. 1 (2000): 4–21.

McFarland, A. S. "Neopluralism." *Annual Review of Political Science* 10, no. 1 (2007): 45–68.

Thatcher, M. "The Development of Policy Network Analyses: From Modest Origins to Overarching Frameworks " *Journal of Theoretical Politics* 10, no. 4 (1998): 389–416.

INDEX